Dan Vogel manages a nearly $200 million advertising budget for one of the Fortune top 100 companies. In his position he works with many beautiful models and actresses.

DAN VOGEL

HOW TO
WIN
WITH WOMEN

Prentice-Hall, Inc., Englewood Cliffs, NJ 07632

Library of Congress Cataloging in Publication Data

Vogel, Dan.
   How to win with women.

   "A Reward Book."
   Bibliography: p.
   Includes index.
   1. Dating (Social customs).   2. Women—Psychology.
3. Interpersonal relations.   I. Title.
HQ801.V64   646.7'7   82-25034
ISBN 0-13-441220-6
ISBN 0-13-441212-5 (PBK)

This book is available at a special discount when ordered in
bulk quantities. Contact Prentice-Hall, Inc., General
Publishing Division, Special Sales, Englewood Cliffs, N.J. 07632

1 2 3 4 5·6 7 8 9 10

ISBN 0-13-441220-6

ISBN 0-13-441212-5 {PBK}

Editorial/production supervision by Alberta Boddy
Cover design by Hal Siegel

Prentice-Hall International, Inc., *London*
Prentice-Hall of Australia Pty. Limited, *Sydney*
Prentice-Hall Canada Inc., *Toronto*
Prentice-Hall of India Private Limited, *New Delhi*
Prentice-Hall of Japan, Inc., *Tokyo*
Prentice-Hall of Southeast Asia Pte. Ltd., *Singapore*
Whitehall Books Limited, Wellington, *New Zealand*
Editora Prentice-Hall do Brasil Ltda., *Rio de Janeiro*

CONTENTS

PREFACE

In case you haven't noticed, women have changed. The woman of the 1980s is unique. She's different. And she's no longer a girl! She knows what she wants and she's determined to have it. And that applies to men. She is assertive, self-confident, and independent. She expects more from her man in a relationship and in bed. Yet for those men who can measure up, it can be the most rewarding experience of their lives. That's because today's woman has much more to offer.

How often have you seen unattractive men (or simply less attractive than you) in the company of beautiful women? Women whose physical beauty marks them as sexually irresistible. And how many times have you found yourself asking, "What does he have that I don't?" Well, you don't need to be earning $40,000 a year or driving a Porsche Targa to attract today's woman. Nor do you need to have the looks of Robert Redford for that matter. So there's no need to make feeble excuses about all the things you don't have. Today's woman is turned on to more than mere good looks or money.

The men who are able to meet and nurture intimate relationships with today's woman are the men who want women the most. Let's face it, you won't meet today's woman sitting home in front of the boob tube or reading the sports page. You have to be sufficiently motivated to get out of your home or apartment if you're ever going to meet the woman of your dreams. If you adopt the attitude that you're interested in meeting women, you'll find the many golden opportunities that are available to you every day.

This book shows you how to take advantage of the opportunities to meet and develop intimate relationships with today's woman. This is not just any book. It bridges the gap between those popular but juvenile books on picking up girls and academic, impractical works by social psychologists. This book is based on practical and proven experiences in winning with women. It shows you how to win with the kind of women you've always dreamed about but never thought you'd be able to meet, much less share intimacy. In fact, you'll learn how to meet more women than you can possibly handle by adopting the principles discussed throughout this book.

So read on and learn these valuable principles. There's a whole world of beautiful women waiting for you. All you need to do is put these principles to work for you. Best wishes.

Dedicated to Today's Women.

Most notably June, Kate, Chris, and Melissa. Also, special thanks to Twila, Warren, Yvett, M. L., Juliette, and Robin. In appreciation of your valuable insights, time, encouragement, and assistance in contributing to the development of this book.

HOW TO WIN WITH WOMEN

CHAPTER ONE

SELF-CONCEPT: THE FIRST STEP

Let's face it, the only way you're going to make contact with women (without the luxury of a formal introduction) is to get out and talk with people. We all know it's not the easiest thing to do. It's much safer staying home and watching the "Monday Night Movie," reading a book, or just plain keeping to yourself. Anything, but anything, is safer than attempting to make contact with a complete stranger—no matter how appealing she is. In order to get started you must believe in yourself. You're going to need some basic confidence in yourself and your ability to make contact. It all starts with a healthy self-concept.

IMPORTANCE OF YOUR SELF-CONCEPT

Recently, I learned about a study that points out the influence of the self-concept in establishing a success profile. A group of Drexel University researchers conducted an experimental class to help college students with serious academic problems. From their experiences, the researchers concluded that IQ, which has long been improperly used to measure intelligence and predict success, may not be to blame for academic failure among many of our nation's college students. Instead, the Drexel researchers concluded that a poor self-concept very often may be at the root of failure.

They found that a student's self-concept influenced his or her behavior in achieving success or failure. Specifically, they observed that students who did not possess a healthy self-concept sought to avoid anxiety through their behavior. This resulted in all the wrong kinds of behavior, such as cutting classes, which in turn contributed to failure and further perpetuated a poor self-concept. The Drexel researchers concluded that an individual's self-concept affects the way he or she approaches everything. It serves as a motivating force that is either positive or negative depending on the state of health of an individual's self-concept.

What does all this have to do with developing intimate relationships? Plenty. It takes a healthy self-concept to muster the courage—the nerve—to attempt contact with a woman you don't know. If you possess a healthy self-concept, you'll accept the risks inherent in attempting contact and set out in a positive manner to accomplish your objectives. On the other hand, if you lack a healthy self-concept, you'll either pass up prime contact opportunities needlessly or undermine encounters by acknowledging defeat at the onset.

That's not all! We project our self-concept to others in the way we act. If you generally like yourself and are reasonably confident in your abilities, women will be comfortable in your presence. It makes it easier for them to enjoy your company. However, if you're not satisfied with yourself and if you lack relatively basic confidence and trust in yourself, you're going to find the going rough. You're making it damned tough for women to be comfortable with you and like you. After all, if you don't like yourself, why should you expect others to like you?

A MATTER OF DEPOSITS AND WITHDRAWALS

Your self-concept is the balance between all the deposits and withdrawals transacted with your personality account throughout the years. The deposits are the successes you've experienced and the encouragement and trust you've received from others. The withdrawals reflect failures, discouragements, and lack of trust. The truth of the matter is that we've all experienced both successes and failures. Although it may seem hard to believe, everyone—and I mean *everyone*—experiences failure at some time. The important element is that if the deposits (successes) exceed the withdrawals (failures) then *voilà*, you'll generally find a healthy self-concept. Unfortunately, a negative self-concept is often a reflection of more numerous, or larger, withdrawals than deposits.

Review your account. Check your balance to see if your self-concept has been blocking productive contact with today's woman. I'd be willing to wager that if you analyze your account carefully, you'll turn up many more (and larger) deposits than withdrawals. Don't dare sell yourself short! It's important to be realistic in assessing yourself and your personal worth. Often, the major cause of a poor self-concept is simply an unrealistic view of what and who you should be. If the ideal you is set too high and out of reach, you'll fail to live up to those unrealistic expectations of yourself. As failures continue to mount under the burden of your self-imposed, unrealistic, unreachable standards, your self-concept will plunge. With it go your chances for success in anything you set out to accomplish.

What's realistic? Perhaps it would be easier to dissolve a few myths and review what isn't realistic first. You don't need to be earning $40,000 a year to make a deposit, or drive an expensive sports car, or speak several languages. You don't need to possess the looks of a movie star, nor do you need to have had the distinction of being class valedictorian. Hell, if that's what is needed to make a deposit, there would be few of us with positive balances in our account. You can make a deposit very easily if you have a few good friends, or an interesting hobby (such as reading, jogging, skiing—it doesn't need to be exotic), or, if others view you as considerate, honest, and a downright decent person. Think this through very carefully. Understand that you're a worthwhile individual. Others would be happy to meet and share your friendship. Just reach out and let your positive balance be felt.

SO WHAT'S EVERYBODY
INTERESTED IN, ANYWAY?

So you don't have the looks of Robert Redford. So you don't dance like John Travolta. So you don't have the gift of tongues like Merv Griffin—so what?

As long as you are an alright person who enjoys the company of others you're in the ballpark. Women are most interested in a man's personality. For the most part, men are interested in many of the same attributes in women with respect to establishing "enduring" relationships. That's not to say that there's no such thing as physical attraction. We all know too well that's simply not the case (particularly with regards to a man's initial interest in a woman). Heaven knows, all we men would just love to share an intimate relationship with Bo Derek. But more important than superficial looks is the core of personality evidenced by your basic warmth, considerateness, sincerity, and genuine interest in others.

Think about this for a moment. How often have you asked yourself, "What does she see in him?" How often have you seen an unattractive man in the company of a beautiful woman? I have seen this many times while walking through the streets of New York City. I'm sure you've witnessed the same in your home town. If it's not a man's looks that have attracted these lovely young women, then what? Wealth? Social position? Perhaps. However, if we fall back on making feeble excuses for all the things we don't have, we're just deluding ourselves. The fact of the matter is these women are attracted to more than a man's good looks or money. They've been hooked on his personality. Personality is as unique as each of us. It's something we all possess and can further develop if that's our wish.

HOW TO BEEF UP
AN UNDERDEVELOPED SELF-CONCEPT

Just as we can develop our minds by getting involved in stimulating mental activity, and build stronger, healthier bodies by exercising regularly, we can beef up our self-concept by employing a few simple principles. Here they are:

MAKE CONTACT: One of the best ways to beef up your self-concept is to make contact with others. Sort of that old prescription "a little of the dog that bit you." As you make contact with others your skills become sharper. You profit from each unique experience. You certainly won't score every time you go to bat. As a matter of fact you won't get a hit every time. But then, nobody does. I've seen Reggie Jackson, the controversial star of the California Angels, strike out on occasion. And Dan Fouts, the star quarterback of the San Diego Chargers, doesn't complete every pass he attempts. Despite occasional setbacks, these superb athletes know they can succeed if they go to bat again or attempt yet another pass.

Likewise, you must believe in your ability to get an occasional hit, complete an occasional pass—and score every so often. However, you'll never get to first base or make a first down if you don't believe enough in yourself to give it a try. So, try! Then, learn from your experiences. Your skills will improve with each experience, and you'll find yourself succeeding more often. In turn, each success will trigger greater confidence, which will encourage you to make more contacts and help you learn more by virtue of increased experiences—and you will succeed again.

One note of caution: Whatever you do, don't fall into the pattern of making the excuse that you are just "plain unlucky" if you run into a few setbacks at first. The only place luck has a role is in the presentation of the opportunity (more specifically, the availability of desirable women for contact). Unless you live in a monastery or on a remote island opportunities should be no problem. The so-called lucky people you see establishing, nurturing, and enjoying intimate relationships with desirable women have been able to capitalize on the same opportunities that are available to you. They've shored up the confidence to make contact and have developed the skills (through experience) to make many of their encounters productive and rewarding.

GIVE YOURSELF A MODEL: Remember, if others can be successful, so can you. Give yourself a model, someone you know who doesn't have any more on the ball than you do. Declare to yourself that, "If he can be successful so can I," and then go to it. A few years ago when I was in the U.S. Navy flight program with the aspirations of becoming a hot-shot carrier pilot, I learned a valuable lesson. Many of my fellow classmates were dropping out of the program like flies. They couldn't handle the sophisticated military aircraft, complete the rigorous ground school training, or accept the pressures of military life. However, I wanted those Navy wings of gold that mark the finest aviators in the world. I wanted the thrill and adventure of carrier take-offs and landings. Above all, I didn't want to go home with my tail between my legs without accomplishing what I had set out to do. So, I set models for myself—people from earlier classes who were achieving success. These were people who I knew were not especially gifted in intelligence or in the possession of unique physical skills. People like myself. I reaffirmed every day that if they could be successful, so could I. I was successful. You can be, too!

SET REALISTIC GOALS: Your chances of ultimate success are much improved if you set realistic goals for yourself. That is, goals you can reach. You're just not going to make new contacts every day or get lured into "the sack" by each new woman you meet. So, why bother to set such unrealistic goals? Failure to achieve these goals only serves to shake your confidence and undermine your enthusiasm. You may be able to establish a new intimacy every month, however! After a while you'll have a cadre of intimate friends. More importantly, with the achievement of your goals, your self-concept will be strengthened and your enthusiasm for making new contacts will be renewed.

Also, it's a good idea to break down your overall goals so that you can guide your progress. For example, your ultimate goal can be broken down into encountering women you believe might make desirable partners. You can then establish as your "subgoal" the objective of making one encounter a week. As your successes grow via the accomplishment of each "subgoal," they will encourage you, and propel you toward achieving your ultimate goal. This holds true no matter what your ultimate goal may be. It works for people in all modes of life, and it can work for you in achieving intimate new relationships.

GIVE OF YOURSELF

Subsequent chapters of this book will give you the information you need to develop intimate new relationships with today's woman. It's up to you to put these new learnings into practice. Perhaps another way to encourage yourself is to realize that you're doing women a favor by making contact. Yes, you've read the last sentence correctly. In addition to doing yourself a favor, you're doing others a favor every time you make contact. In pure, simple terms you aren't going to be the only one who profits from a new relationship. After all, you'll be satisfying some basic needs of others as well. Remember, you're a unique person with many desirable attributes and, as such, many women will profit from sharing a relationship with you.

If you still feel any trepidation, you might consider that today's woman will be impressed by virtue of your attempt to make contact. Most folks recognize that it takes courage to attempt contact with a complete stranger. It is something that we all have wanted desperately to do, at one time or another, but didn't. Women will most likely admire your courage. Also, you'll find most women flattered by your approach. Your attempt to make meaningful contact indicates that you feel a person is desirable, worthy of attention, and important. That's flattery.

So give it a try. Now it's up to you to learn these valuable principles, put them into practice, and enjoy your successes.

CHAPTER TWO

HOW TO GET WOMEN INTERESTED IN YOU

Now that you've reviewed your personality account, you should be convinced you're a worthwhile, desirable individual who has much to offer today's woman. You should be raring to tackle the world of opportunities that is out there for the asking. However, one question remains: How do you get today's woman interested in you?· How do you get women to notice and appreciate your many fine attributes? After all, we all know the value of a diamond, yet many of us might fail to recognize its inherent worth before it is cut and displayed. Likewise, your most important attributes must be carefully brought out and displayed if your value as a potential intimate partner is to be appreciated.

Getting today's woman interested in you is not as difficult as one might think if you are aware of a few basic sales principles. The first and perhaps most important to remember is that a woman must profit in some way, she must gain some value before she'll buy. Let's face it, during any encounter you're selling! In this case the product a woman will be buying is you and your unique personality. You don't need to come on strong and try to impress her with your Pierre Cardin belt or Gucci shoes. The days of Willy Loman and the hard sell are over. The key today is in being *other directed.* In other words, the best way to get today's woman interested in you is to demonstrate that you're genuinely interested in her. In order to sell yourself you have to satisfy the needs of others first. In doing so you are providing real value and both parties profit.

Let's put this in perspective. Review a few of your own experiences. Over the years I'm sure you've come into contact with a wide variety of personality types. I'd be willing to bet the one you like least is the so-called "stuck-up" personality. That's the type who's so involved in herself she makes all those she comes into contact with feel unimportant or, worse yet, worthless. On the other hand, there's the "other directed" personality. That's the type who appears to be more interested in you and what you have to say than she is about tooting her own horn. That's the type you come away from feeling good about yourself, her, and the budding relationship. It's rare to come away satisfied from an encounter with the "stuck-up" personality, but it is even more rare when you don't come away totally satisfied when you've been with an "other directed" person.

THE LAW OF RECIPROCITY

There's a second basic principle: the law of reciprocity. It provides insight into how we may benefit by putting the needs of today's woman before our own. This principle has been evidenced in innumerable encounters and is as irrefutable as Einstein's theory of relativity. Simply stated, as you give value to others they in turn feel obligated to satisfy your needs. It's sort of an unwritten contract among people, a subtle version of "you scratch my back and I'll scratch yours."

Here's a simple illustration of how the law of reciprocity can work for you. A friend of mine was lined up at the bank to cash a check during the busy lunch hour. Despite the fact that he was several feet from the head of the line, he noticed that the teller, a beautiful young woman, had become distressed by the rude behavior of the bank's lunch-hour clientele. As he came closer to the head of the line, he watched her grow more and more sullen, withdrawn, and cool towards those angry customers. This was the law of reciprocity operating negatively. Determined to brighten the lovely teller's disposition, he decided to put the law of reciprocity to work for him. So, he greeted her with a warm smile and "hello" when he reached the window. She responded with a slight nod. He quickly sensed it would take more than his friendly greeting to warm her up. So he began sympathizing with her about her difficult predicament dealing with the gruff, impatient customers. It didn't take long before she opened up and told him how distressful her day had been. Noting that she was beginning to thaw to his interest in her, he complimented her with a broad smile on her ability to keep cool and told her how lovely and composed she looked. The outcome was predictable. She returned his warm smile and thanked him.

My friend returned to her window later that day during a less hectic hour. The teller recognized him immediately and greeted him with an enthusiastic hello and a smile. He sensed from her behavior that she had been hoping to see him again. Caught up in their mutual interest in each other, they arranged to have dinner together. Today their relationship has grown into genuine intimacy. That's the law of reciprocity at its best.

BASIC NEEDS

Dr. Abraham Maslow, a noted clinical psychologist, catalogued the hierarchy of human needs. While we're not interested in reviewing all the psychological ramifications, an understanding of Maslow's hierarchy can provide insights into identifying the interests of others. As such, it can help make your encounters more productive and rewarding. Basically, Maslow found that an individual will try to satisfy his or her most elementary needs. At that time, more sophisticated needs take control of and direct our behavior until they, too, are satisfied.

1. The most elementary needs identified by Maslow are the "physiological" needs, which occupy the first rung of the ladder. These needs are hunger, thirst, health, rest, shelter, and so forth. As you can imagine, these needs will command our energies until they are fully satisfied. Let's face it, to the man stranded in the desert, nothing—absolutely nothing—is more important than water.

2. The next rung up the ladder is the need for safety, as evidenced by a desire for order, basic safety, job security, stability, and peace of mind.

3. Thirdly, come social needs. These are the needs of love and belonging. It is on this rung that men and women thirst to be understood, accepted, and popular. It is on this rung that people seek to belong and are compelled to pursue and achieve meaningful, intimate relationships.

4. On the uppermost rung are esteem needs. These can be divided into the "self-esteem" needs, such as the drive for knowledge, confidence, sense of accomplishment, and mastery of one's job. The other set of esteem needs are those that impinge upon one's reputation: prestige, status, recognition, importance, and understanding.

An understanding of this hierarchy of needs can give you a competitive advantage in getting women interested in you. Here's a vignette that dramatizes the importance of understanding the needs of others in developing a productive relationship:

Jack and Ted both happen to notice the flashy redhead from their positions on opposite sides of the dance floor. She was gorgeous: tall, with a provocative, full-bodied figure, and she danced superbly. She enjoyed one dance after another with each of the men who strode up to invite her. After watching from his position for nearly forty-five minutes, Ted walked up to Meg, the redhead and object of his desire, and invited her to dance. Unfortunately, Meg was taking a breather from her continual dancing, and despite the fact that she found Ted attractive, she wanted to sit for awhile and rest. Ted took this for rejection and went off to the bar to sulk.

At about the same time, Jack approached Meg for a dance. However, Jack recognized that Meg was simply tired and asked her if she would care to sit and join him for a drink. Meg accepted his invitation gratefully. Jack learned that Meg loved to dance, but she also enjoyed sitting and talking over a drink—getting to know people. She didn't feel as though she could really talk over the loud music on the dance floor or get to know her partners. Jack also learned that Meg had other interests she enjoyed every bit as much as dancing. What Jack learned was that Meg was more than a fascinating dancer and that she wanted others to know and respect her for her many talents. She wanted others to know the real Meg: competent legal stenographer, outstanding skier, and a woman who enjoyed intellectual challenges and activities. She was not just the flashy redhead on the dance floor.

Unfortunately for the other men who came into contact with Meg on the dance floor, they didn't realize that Meg had important social and esteem needs she needed fulfilled. Jack did, and he succeeded in achieving intimacy with Meg where others had failed.

HOW TO SATISFY
THE NEEDS OF TODAY'S WOMEN

The first order of business is to cultivate a personal style that projects a genuine interest in others. Your style, or behavior, projects your feelings and attitudes towards women. It is who and what you are, not what you say. Today's woman can easily tell if you're genuinely interested in her or rather in satisfying your own needs. You can't fake it, so don't bother to try. If your words don't betray you, your body, actions, or eyes will.

Basically, there are two styles from which to choose in attempting to sell yourself and develop relationships. The first is "genuine interest and caring" for others. It's a style that says to women: "I value you for who and what you are, and I want to know more about you." It's a style that exudes warmth and tenderness. It's "other directed." Because it's non-threatening, it creates a safe, friendly climate conducive to the growth of genuine intimacy.

The second style is destructive. It's the Machiavellian or manipulative style of behavior. This style attempts to control others. While it may be successful in winning you an occasional "one night stand," it won't get you to first base when it comes to establishing more intimate, lasting relationships.

BE GENUINE AND CARING

Here are some ways you can cultivate a style of genuine interest and caring for others:

EMPATHIZE WITH HER: Put yourself in her shoes. This will help you understand her needs and feelings. Moreover, it will provide value to her in that she will come to feel that you genuinely appreciate, value, and understand her. Just like Meg, everyone wants to be appreciated, valued, and understood. You can improve your empathy quotient by paraphrasing her comments, asking open-ended questions (questions that require more than a simple yes or no answer), or expressing your appreciation for her point of view. Most important, abide by the golden rule and treat any woman you meet as you would like to be treated.

ASSUME THE BEST: Much criticism has been heaped on the role of assumption. The argument goes that if you're making assumptions about what and who others are, you're really not getting to know and understand who the other person is. Assumptions, like stereotypes, are most often inaccurate. Let's face it, we can't hope to accurately evaluate another's personality in just the first few minutes of an encounter. So, assumptions can trip you in discovering another's real personality. For all those reasons, we're told assuming is taboo.

On the other hand, you can make your assumptions work in your favor if you make positive assumptions about the qualities of the women you meet. The famous German philosopher Goethe wrote: "Treat people as if they are already what they ought to be and you make it possible for them to act their best." If you assume your new acquaintances are friendly, warm, considerate, and interesting, chances are they will act and become that way with you. Moreover, you will have contributed to getting today's woman interested in you.

As you become "other directed," you'll find that you'll release more of you. Instead of freezing in a social situation, you'll begin to thaw, thereby releasing your own personality into the mix of things. You could kindle the spark that will lead to genuine intimacy.

CHAPTER THREE

HOW TO TALK
WITH WOMEN
ABOUT PRACTICALLY
ANYTHING

One of the most productive ways to demonstrate your interest in women, and stimulate their interest in you, is through the simple act of conversation. That's obvious, you say. As strange as it may seem, however, many people really don't understand the true nature of conversation. To many it amounts to nothing more than serving as a sounding board for others. To still others, conversation is saying your piece regardless of the topic under discussion or the interests of others. However, according to my dictionary, conversation is an "exchange." It's the mutual give and take of ideas, philosophies, observations, and so forth. In other words, conversation is sharing.

It's simply not conversation to stand mute like a part of the furnishings while another person's talk fills the surrounding vacuum. Instead, you need to sprinkle your thoughts like a gentle rain on a seedbed if a budding relationship is going to grow strong.

The importance of conversation to the development of a relationship with today's woman is dramatized by the following encounter between a former co-worker of mine, whom I'll call Ron Mullen, and my favorite cousin, Jane. Ron is a twenty-eight-year-old licensed pharmacist who works in research and development of new proprietary drug products. His intellect is rather significant. Jane is a stock broker with a fair intellect herself and a lust for life that is evidenced by a broad range of interests. She's certainly one of "today's" women. Both are strikingly attractive.

One afternoon Ron was in my office, updating me on the status of a few new product ideas and getting my opinion as to whether they were marketable and worth pursuing in the lab. It so happened that Jane gained entry into my office while my meeting with Ron was in progress. She invited me down to the tennis courts to substitute for her double's partner. When she saw Ron she was immediately attracted to him. In order to help my cousin, I arranged a barbecue and invited a few couples so that Ron and Jane could get to know each other a little better. (I must admit it was Jane's idea, not mine.)

I carefully selected a diverse group of people to promote conversation. With that, it was up to Ron and Jane to evaluate whether there was a mutual chemistry between the two. Well, on the evening of the barbecue Jane started the conversation talking about a book she had read recently about Alaska. She said she'd like to do some more traveling. Everyone but Ron took part in the conversation and related his or her travel experiences, books and magazines about far off and exotic places, and travelogues he or she had seen.

Sensing that Ron might be somewhat bashful, Jane pulled him aside and began talking about the current situation in the Middle East, soliciting his opinions on a topic that most people are familiar with. Still no response. Jane, fancying herself as a good conversationalist, employed all the techniques she had cultivated over the years. Still no response. As dynamic and interesting as Jane is, she quickly became bored with Ron and left his side to socialize with others.

As the evening progressed Ron went his own way—without Jane. Curious about the outcome of their encounter, I asked Jane how things went with Ron. She responded, "It didn't go." It appeared to Jane that as handsome as Ron Mullen is on the outside, he really is very plain on the inside. Unfortunately, his interests and conversation were limited only to work. In an effort to advance his career and make his mark on the world he had failed to cultivate other interests, as well as an ability to converse on any subject but pharmacology. In short, Ron was not very interesting to Jane.

BRING OUT THE
CONVERSATIONALIST IN YOU

You can see it's important to broaden and cultivate your interests. It will make you more interesting in the eyes of today's woman and enable you to better appreciate the women with whom you come into contact. This doesn't mean that you need to be one of the great Western minds, and cultivated with a breadth of knowledge that is encyclopedic in scope. Nor does it mean that you need to force-feed your memory with tons of idle facts, figures, scripts, or anecdotes. What it does mean is that you should attempt to become familiar with a few general topics (one of which could very well be yourself) to stimulate conversation and to provide a basis by which women can come to know the real you. Here are a few suggestions that might serve you well:

READ

Millions of people read for the pure pleasure and entertainment value it provides. In fact, the publishing industry has grown into a multi-billion-dollar business to fill America's almost insatiable desire for good reading material. People generally enjoy conversing with others who share their interests in books or the subjects they enjoy.

Of course, if you don't enjoy reading, don't force it. If you're not going to "be yourself," you'll never really enjoy the resultant relationship. On the other hand, if you're like most people who enjoy reading but just haven't been able to find the time—make the time. Take note of those items, articles, thoughts, and subjects that interest you. They'll help you better understand yourself as well as expand your horizons and your ability to converse freely with today's woman.

What should you read? This is not an English course with a long listing of required reading. You certainly don't need to read Tolstoy's *War and Peace* or Mann's *The Beloved Returns*. There are few women who can or would ever enjoy discussing these books. So what do you read? Just about anything you fancy. Pick up magazines and books on subjects that are of interest to you. It could be specialized subjects such as gardening or Chinese cooking, or broad subjects and topics that you'll find in newspapers. It might be a good idea to read a best seller now and then. They are often the topic of conversation in many encounters and social circles.

GET OUT TO THE MOVIES

Most women are fascinated with movies and movie stars. Movies have entertained millions of people and are the focus of countless hours of conversation.

The movie industry and Hollywood glitter have a mystique that draws people like a two-ton magnet. So take in a movie now and then. You'll often find it will broaden your awareness of personalities and issues, which alone could be very helpful to you. Moreover, it will help you relax, which in this rapidly changing and complex world is alone worth the cost of admission. More importantly, it will give you something you could probably share in a new encounter.

EXCITING EVENTS

"I was flying back to home base, tucked tightly into my squad leader when all of a sudden . . ." You've probably experienced interesting and exciting events during your life. Most women enjoy hearing others talk about their experiences, providing they don't come off like braggarts. And while you probably haven't ejected from a military aircraft during a flameout, I'll be willing to wager you've enjoyed your fair share of rather interesting experiences.

Perhaps you've delivered an important speech on a controversial topic that won converts to your position, or attended a Rolling Stones concert given to a few hundred thousand screaming fans, or experienced a blowout while driving on an Interstate highway during which your cool head and quick reflexes averted a potential catastrophe, or visited the Smithsonian's National Aerospace Museum in Washington, D.C., where you touched and examined a lunar rock retrieved from one of the last manned missions to the moon.

Far out you say? Not really. If you think back over the years you'll probably be able to come up with several interesting topics for conversation that today's woman can either relate to or would just enjoy sharing with you. The key is that the experience doesn't have to be exciting to be of interest to others. It could simply be your hobby, whether it's Tuesday night bowling or caring for a pet iguana. My grandmother serves as an excellent example that the experience need not be exciting. Picture this: A white-haired old lady of seventy-three, permanently stooped from working all her life over a sewing machine, seated on a park bench alternately knitting and admiring ducks swimming in the clear blue pond. Along comes a distinguished looking gentleman who's not so young himself (about eighty). He takes his place on the park bench and leans forward on his cane as he admires the ducks as they zigzag across the pond. The conversation went something like this:

> **GRANDMOTHER:** "Lovely day, isn't it?" She looks down through the glasses delicately balanced on her nose at her knitting.
>
> **DISTINGUISHED GENTLEMAN:** "It certainly is." He quickly glances over at my grandmother and then back to the ducks on the pond.

GRANDMOTHER: "I'm knitting a sweater for my great grandson. My granddaughter has a 6-month-old little boy." She momentarily stops knitting to look over to the distinguished gentleman and cast a smile.

DISTINGUISHED GENTLEMAN: "Oh ... that's interesting." He gazes at my grandmother, who's stooped busily over her knitting.

GRANDMOTHER: "Yes." She places her knitting down on her lap and looks over at the distinguished gentleman. "They live in Boston ...."

And from that discourse flowed a warm exchange of feelings and views. From sharing springs forth a relationship. So you see, here's proof positive that your experience need not be terribly exciting. It is my grandmother's warmth, personality, and caring attitude that "hooked" others. The conversation, and in particular the experience, is merely the vehicle for gaining attention. Try it some time recounting a hobby, activity, or experience. It works best when it provides some insight into your personality. Remember, it worked for my grandmother, and it can work for you.

CURRENT EVENTS

You can't turn on a radio or TV, pick up a newspaper, or enter a social circle without getting a fill of current events. It might be a headline shouting the ever growing tide of inflation, or another tale of woe about unemployment ... to name just a couple. You'll find today's woman is interested in current events. She's eager to express her views. Moreover, she's probably eager to learn your views on these important topics since they affect her standard and quality of life.

If you want to be included in conversations and make new acquaintances with today's women, you should be familiar with what's going on in the world and even your own town. Make it a practice to tune into the news occasionally. Also, follow-up with newspapers or news magazines for more detailed information on the subjects that are of particular interest to you. Be prepared to share your views.

SPORTS ARE OKAY

Sports is another topic of immense interest to the American public—and that includes women. This is evident by the ever-increasing gate receipts at sporting events, of which women contribute a significant share. Try to buy your way into season tickets and you'll find yourself on a waiting list that spans many seasons in many cities. And the major topic of conversation around the water cooler on Monday morning among both men and women is generally the outcome of Sunday's football game.

Such is the appeal of and the preoccupation with sports. Depending on the season, millions of women will "root, root, root for the home team," whether it be football, hockey, gymnastics, or any of the televised sports. So, if sports are of interest to you, you've a tailor-made opportunity to stimulate and participate in conversation with many new encounters.

You don't have to become bogged down with needless facts and statistics, although if you're predisposed to such they could serve to support your point of view. All you really have to do is follow the latest developments in your favorite sport(s). Take in a game now and then at the stadium or in the comfort of your favorite armchair. Scan the sports pages to keep in touch with reports and analyses of noteworthy events. Then join in on talk about the home team's performance in the last game or the exploits, either on or off the field, of one of the team's or sport's superstars. You might even venture your prognosis about the outcome of an upcoming game or match. The possibilities are limitless.

By all means, you don't have to limit yourself to armchair sports. There's a revolution taking place across this dynamic country of ours. It's the rise and continued growth of the "Me generation." It spans all age groups—not just youths. And today's woman is playing a major role in this revolution. Specifically, the "Me generation" deals with people who are interested in their own personal grooming, health, and enjoyment; people who are interested in getting on with the business of living and reaching out for the "gusto" in life.

The "Me generation" is into tennis, mountaineering, jogging, hang gliding, backpacking, sky diving, canoeing, paddleball, raquetball, and even foosball. They jump and stretch with Jack LaLaine, immerse themselves in yoga with Lilias Forman, take to the beaches in droves to bask in the sun and swim in the surf. They're into their own physical well being and activities. They enjoy exchanging ideas and opinions on their favorite activities.

Consider Kim Rainville. She's up at the crack of dawn every morning and runs approximately six miles around the reservoir in Central Park in New York City. Kim really enjoys her activity and could spend endless hours talking about the merits of this or that running shoe, what and how much one should eat before a race, or the psychology of racing. She's just as content to discuss the sheer pleasure one gets from running free out of doors.

So, if you can be counted as a member of the growing ranks of the "Me generation," you might very well share your activity with women. If you've been postponing your own interests in favor of making a living or plodding through school, perhaps it's time for you to change your lifestyle. It could very well help you get to know today's woman.

DREAMS OF FARAWAY PLACES

Who doesn't enjoy travel? We all work and plan how we're going to spend our all-too-fleeting annual vacation. While we all don't get to travel, most of us dream of it. We dream of South Sea breezes, dancing under the moonlight in some exotic faraway place, sipping Pina Coladas during the day and beholding the monuments of nature and mankind.

Travel is a prime subject of many a conversation. I can tell you from firsthand experience that women enjoy sharing travel experiences. Perhaps it's because today's woman enjoys reminiscing about the good times she's enjoyed away from the pressures of everyday living. Whatever the reason, you can share a conversation with today's woman by simply comparing notes on your travels. Talk about the people you've met, the sights you've seen, the differences in the way of life of people from other parts of the world (or this country for that matter).

You can be an interesting conversationalist. All it takes is a little preparation. The payoff is big. In time you'll be able to move in and out of conversation with women easily. Keep a conversation flowing with a new encounter. And in time you'll find yourself easing into rewarding relationships with today's women.

TAKE NOTE AND LISTEN

"Take note and listen." You've probably heard this advice before and you're smart if you heed it. Good listeners make better conversationalists. And, as we've discussed, good conversationalists generally are able to get closer to and establish intimate relationships with today's woman. The reason is not difficult to understand. No one is appreciated more than a person who cares enough to really listen. Listening evidences interest in others. It indicates a desire to understand and get to know others. Listening is truly "other directed," and it nourishes the self-esteem of others. It serves to make the women you come in contact with feel more important and appreciated, which unlocks doors to new relationships and genuine intimacy.

Ben Franklin, one of the founders of our country and a great statesman, dazzled royalty in Europe with his ability as a conversationalist. In fact, he was able to mix freely with royalty and get them to support our emerging nation. But he wrote: "The wit of conversation consists more in finding it in others than showing a great deal of it yourself." In other words, Ben Franklin knew one of the most important principles of good conversation. He was a good listener.

Unfortunately, many people believe they're good listeners just because they have two ears. They make the common mistake of confusing hearing with listening. In reality, the two are miles apart. Listening is not a passive state, but an active one that requires intense concentration. Listening is an attempt to understand not just the words, but also the attitudes, feelings, body language, and tone of others.

BARRIERS TO LISTENING

Few people listen well. For many it's nothing more than the proverbial "in one ear and out the other." For others, listening is blocked by predispositions and assumptions. The reason so many people have difficulty listening is because it is not a natural process, like hearing. Don't despair, however. Good listening skills can be developed.

One of the first steps toward becoming a better listener and conversationalist is to be aware of some of the common barriers. They're habits we unconsciously develop over the years that interfere with our ability to truly learn about others and make them feel important. Among the more common barriers are: assumption, filtration, distraction, interruption, and focusing on facts.

ASSUMPTION: All too often people make assumptions about others based on common stereotypes or their own experiences. They'll assume what others are going to say and tune out the intended message. Making assumptions about what you think women will say will often prevent you from really learning and understanding what it is they intended for you to know. To overcome premature evaluation, try to withhold making assumptions until others finish talking. Then, ask questions or ask if you might interpret what you believe they said to ensure you understand their attitudes and feelings correctly.

FILTRATION: Filtration is nothing more than being caught up in your own prejudices. You really don't hear what others are telling you because you're too involved in your own predispositions. For example, Tony and Yvette meet at a cocktail party. They're both attracted to each other right from the start. Yvette invites Tony back to her apartment for something to eat and a few drinks. Although Yvette wants nothing more than to get to know Tony better and enjoy a few more hours with him, Tony interprets her invitation as a sexual advance. When they get to Yvette's apartment, Tony becomes sexually aggressive and is rebuffed by Yvette. What he failed to do is really listen and understand what Yvette wanted. Growing up in an environment where men (not women) took the initiative, Tony failed to listen and understand what Yvette really wanted. As a result he undermined what could have been a rewarding relationship.

DISTRACTION: We can think much faster than we can speak. In fact, we can think four to five times faster. Unfortunately, many times we use our excess thinking power to come up with a response to another while she's still talking! This prevents us from hearing what she says or more specifically understanding what she's saying. The excess thinking power is further compounded by our desire to say our piece or come off as appearing knowledgeable. The only way to overcome this habit is to concentrate—really concentrate—on what others have to say. If your mind is going to engage in mental gymnastics, put your excess thinking power to good use. Think about what she is telling you—not what you are going to say.

INTERRUPTING: Your mouth was not made for listening. If you're going to hear what women are attempting to tell you, you'll need to overcome the urge to interrupt. Not only does interrupting prevent you from hearing, but it is downright rude. If you find yourself speaking before others are finished, try counting to three before you speak. This will provide ample time for others to finish speaking and will serve to fill any clumsy voids in the conversation. As well, it will keep you from stepping on her lines.

FOCUS ON FACTS: Words don't tell the whole story. To really hear what women are saying you must be aware of their vocal tone, facial expressions, and body language. You need to search out their feelings and attitudes and not just listen for the facts.

If you find yourself engaging in one of these barriers, don't be disturbed. You're not alone. Most people have developed two or more of these common habits. Now that you are aware of them, you can work to overcome these barriers and lay the foundation for improving your skills as a listener and conversationalist. All it takes is concentration, awareness, patience, and practice.

HOW TO IMPROVE YOUR LISTENING SKILLS

Here are some principles that can serve you well in improving your listening skills:

GET WOMEN TO TALK ABOUT THEIR INTERESTS: If there's one thing others are interested in, it's themselves. Deep inside every woman is the "real me" dying to be discovered and appreciated. She is a person with hopes, fears, aspirations, and desires, all of which she'd love to tell you about if you only gave her a little encouragement. Every woman desires to feel important and wanted. When you get women to talk about themselves or their interests you really make them feel important.

To draw the woman you meet at the bus stop out of her shell, get her to talk about her interests. All you have to do is ask her a few simple questions, and she'll do the rest if you continue to stoke the flame. A few of the areas you may get her to talk about include, but are not limited to, areas we discussed earlier: hobbies, work, books, current events, the weather, and so on. Here are a few sample questions to get her started:

- "What do you think of this weather we've been having?"
- "What do you enjoy most/least about your work?"
- "What's that book you're reading? It has an interesting cover."

Whatever her personal interests, when you get today's woman to talk about herself, and her likes and dislikes, you get insights into her personal values, attitudes, and feelings. In doing so you'll gain her trust and open up new possibilities for intimacy. So forget about yourself when meeting and talking with new contacts. Look carefully to pick up clues about her interests and get her to talk about them.

ENCOURAGE WOMEN THROUGH THE USE OF POSITIVE BODY GESTURES: What you don't say may have a more lasting impression than words. Gestures that show others you are interested in listening serve to lubricate the conversation. Women are particularly attuned to interpreting body language. In fact, studies show that women listen differently than men. While men focus on words, or what is expressed verbally, women listen to how the message is stated. They're sensitive and quick to pick up tone, inflection and body language. You should use body gestures that communicate real interest in others. Here are a few:

- *Maintain Eye Contact:* This provides important reassurance to others. It shows you are interested in them, and you feel they are important. One way to improve eye contact is to make a conscious decision to look women in the eyes and then lock in.
- *Nod Agreement:* If you agree with or approve of another's position, let her know by nodding your head in agreement. This reinforces her sense of worth and will serve to stimulate her to talk more about her interests or position. It helps establish the mutual trust that will contribute to genuine

intimacy. As a bond of trust is established, she'll begin to share her true feelings with you in an unrestrained outpouring that will signal the opportunity for real intimacy. Everyone craves approval, and your nodding signals that approval.

- *Face And Lean Toward Others:* This shows that you are attracted to and interested in what she is saying. It also cordons you off from others and any distractions that might be present to establish privacy.
- *Smile:* A smile can help to reduce any nervousness or fear. It shows that you are friendly and establishes a basic warmth. Also, it shows that you accept her.
- *Be Open:* Keep your arms uncrossed and frequently show the palms of your hands. You might even employ touching techniques. These gestures establish that you are open and help create an atmosphere of mutual trust. Additionally, they help tear down any artificial barriers that may have consciously or subconsciously sprung up as defense mechanisms to protect against potential rejection.

ASK OPEN-ENDED QUESTIONS: Open-ended questions are designed to elicit more than a simple "Yes" or "No" answer. They require an explanation, and they encourage and invite others to continue speaking. Moreover, they demonstrate your interest in another's opinions, feelings, and attitudes. They show concern and contribute to arousing a woman's interest in you.

If you don't ask open-ended questions, you risk ending a potentially intimate relationship with a quick "No" before it ever gets off the ground. One way to make sure your questions are open-ended is to begin them with "how" or "what". Here are a few examples:

- "How did you get involved in dancing?"
- "What are your life goals?"
- "What do you think is the reason for the book's success?"
- "What do you like most about living in the city?"

- "How would you define success?"
- "How are you planning to spend your vacation?"
- "What do you value most in your relationships?"

Barbara Walters, newswoman and celebrity, uses an open-ended questioning technique designed to bring out peoples' attitudes, values, opinions, and feelings in a very non-threatening way. She asks indirect questions that are really fun to answer such as:

- "If you could be anyone in history, whom might you choose and why?"
- "If you came into a million dollar inheritance, what would you do with your life?"
- "What famous person would you like to be shipwrecked on a deserted island with, and why that particular individual?"

These open-ended questions get women to talk about and reveal more about themselves. You'll learn about their wishes, dreams, and desires. In doing so, you'll be kindling their interest in you through the care, interest, and concern your listening shows them.

RESTATE AND INTERPRET: When you restate another's opinion or interpret what she has said you're giving her a psychological boost. It says that you feel what she has to say is of interest and importance, and that makes today's woman feel important, unlocking new doors to intimacy.

By applying each of these principles you will be able to talk with today's woman about almost anything. Women will find you more interesting and enjoy conversing with and being in your company. They will develop a basic trust that will help you gain their hearts.

CHAPTER FOUR

HOW TO HANDLE INTRODUCTIONS

Now you're prepared to engage any woman in conversation. You have a catalog of interesting topics filed conveniently inside your memory center ready to be retrieved automatically during a conversation. You also know how to be a good listener to gain the trust and interest of new acquaintances. The question is: "How do you make contact with desirable women?"

Perhaps the most frequent way of making contact is through the third party introduction. Simply stated, you are introduced to someone by a mutual friend or acquaintance. Whether it be at work, school, a party, or at the local watering hole, we all invariably get the opportunity to expand our circle of friends through third party introductions. These introductions generally go something like this: "John, I'd like you to meet Claire. She's in my biology class . . ."

If you are fortunate enough to receive an introduction, you have a solid base for building a new relationship. Third party introductions are nearly always draped in background information regarding her past and/or current affiliations, interests, employment, travel, and so forth that can be used to open a conversation. Here's an example of how you can use the third party introduction to your advantage:

THIRD
PARTY: "John, I'd like you to meet Claire, she just moved into the neighborhood."

JOHN: "Well, hi Claire. I'm pleased to welcome you to the neighborhood."

CLAIRE: "Thank you John. I'm pleased to join this community. Just about everything I enjoy—the theatre, movies, bike paths—are within walking distance of my apartment. And the people are so friendly!"

At this point, John has several areas he can pursue. He might concentrate on a mutual interest:

"The availability of big fine theaters, that's what sold me on this neighborhood. Just last Saturday I took in "A Chorus Line" at the ..."

Or he might search for additional background information. "Yes, I agree with you":

"Where are you from?"
"Who else have you met?"
"Where is your apartment?"
"Have you had an opportunity to take in a show as of yet?"
"When did you move in?"

This conversation can continue until both John and Claire have sufficient background information about each other to determine whether they want to maintain, cultivate, or terminate the relationship. This same opportunity is open to you when you're presented with any introduction. When the general background gathering exchange begins to slow down, you can shift the conversation to one or more of the areas we discussed in the last chapter.

RULES OF THE ROAD

In those few instances where the third party introduction does not include background information, don't despair. You can easily scratch about the surface on your own. One suggestion is simply to initiate a discussion about the person who made the introduction. After all, he or she is a common denominator to both parties. From that initial discussion each party can begin to expand his or her search for background information and then exchange views and opinions on areas of mutual interest. Here are several important rules of the road to help you make each third party introduction more productive:

DON'T ARGUE

Avoid arguments at any cost. No one ever really wins an argument. Egos become entangled, listening ceases, and with that any hope for establishing an intimate relationship is lost. Keep away from controversial subjects during the initial encounter. Sufficient trust, understanding, and patience hasn't had the time to develop and become established to tolerate an argument.

Remember, a conversation isn't two rams stubbornly butting heads to prove supremacy. The objective isn't for one to win and the other to lose. In that type of situation both parties lose. Instead, the initial encounter should be a mutual sharing and searching for information that will help you evaluate your potential new partner and relationship.

DON'T BE A KNOW-IT-ALL

You've probably run into the type. He knows (or more appropriately stated, thinks he knows) everything about anything and is quick to pontificate on any subject at length. I find this type of individual to be extremely obnoxious, and most women share my sentiments.

The "know-it-all" carries a suffocating air of superiority. He appears to be saying, "I'm smarter than you." Also, instead of catering to another's need to feel important, he undermines it! Few women appreciate or care to be in the company of a "know-it-all."

DON'T BE PASSIVE

Certainly you should listen. However, listening is not a passive activity. If you are just going to stand mutely by, your new encounter might as well be talking to a wall. So be active. Ask questions to keep the conversation flowing, and show your interest in her.

For a helpful example of an active listener, all you need to do is turn on your TV and observe one of the popular talk show hosts. Johnny Carson, Merv Griffin, Phil Donahue, Barbara Walters—are each pros. They know how to talk with people, make them feel as though they've something important to say. They all ask questions that require an explanation, and they are quick to pick out topics of interest and get their guests to talk more on those subjects.

In addition to asking questions, these talk show hosts communicate with body language (a raised eyebrow, warm smile, touching, etc.) thereby communicating that they're genuinely interested in their guests and what they have to say. All these activities cater to the needs of the individual and promote mutual respect. And respect is an important building block in establishing a meaningful and productive relationship with today's woman.

DON'T BE CONCERNED WITH YOURSELF

Primping, looking about the room, any extraneous activity while she is talking to you will lead her to believe you're not really interested in what she has to say. So give your undivided attention to today's woman lest she deservedly give you the brush off.

DON'T BE AFRAID

Although we've talked about this earlier, it's important enough to bear repeating. If you are going to proceed timidly, you will make others very uncomfortable. Women are quick to sense discomfort, just as animals can sense fear or hostility in people. Moreover, when one is in obvious discomfort, it makes the situation tenuous for the other.

Furthermore, you could find yourself becoming even more uptight. Fear plays on itself and can get out of control. As an illustration, I remember walking with my boyhood friends down the long dark alleyway behind our homes in the dead of a summer night. We'd talk about vampires, ghouls, and werewolves in an attempt to prove that we were not afraid of the dark. All of a sudden, one of us would let out a primeval scream of terror and bolt for the end of the alleyway some three hundred yards away. Then all pandemonium would break loose as each of us ran as fast as our legs could carry us, propelled by fear of the unknown, the dark, and the sounds of our own feet and screams. This illustration is not meant to suggest that you might turn into a screaming fool as a result of your encounter, but you could "choke" and fail to hear what others are telling you in word and action, or fail to let the real you emerge during an encounter.

This isn't intended to paralyze you with fear regarding a contact with today's woman. There is nothing to fear because you have nothing to lose. After all you can't lose something you don't have. If you are anything like most men, your ego is strong enough to handle rejection, and that's the very thing that most men do fear—rejection.

We all face rejection in some form or other on a frequent basis. Rejection *doesn't* mean that there's something wrong with you, that you are a failure! My job brings me in contact with hundreds of beautiful models and actresses, each vying for a spot in a television commercial for one of the products I market. They're among the most beautiful women you've ever seen—thick lustrous hair; full bodies; shapely figures; picture-book smiles; perfect, pearly teeth; big, expressive eyes; warm, engaging personalities; and the list goes on. Yet for every twenty women who audition, only one will be selected. The other nineteen will be rejected despite all their beauty, poise, and talent. Is there anything wrong with those that are rejected? No, not at all. Do they fear being rejected? It certainly doesn't appear that they're afraid. Day after day they pick themselves up after an audition, hail a cab, and hurry on down to another audition across town.

Likewise, you probably won't get close to every woman with whom you'd hope to cultivate a relationship. Nevertheless, as you experience more encounters, your social skills and ability to establish productive new relationships will improve. If nothing more, you'll learn there's nothing to fear and that alone will improve your prospects.

DON'T BE ARTIFICIAL

You really don't fool people—not for long. The objective is to get really close to women, establish an intimate relationship, and share feelings, hopes, and aspirations. Deception, while it may afford you a brief advantage, is bound to be discovered. And when deception is discovered, hostility could erupt and the relationship is almost certain to sour and terminate. A recent box office film success called "Breaking Away" illustrates this point. The hero, a young "townie," wishes to win the heart of a college girl. Yet, because he does not attend college, he feels he is not up to the coed's usual boyfriends— bright, athletic college fellows who command the town's streets in their expensive and flashy sports cars. Our hero, a bicycle racer, poses as an Italian exchange student and wins his heart's desire through his suave and charming European ways. As might be expected, the girl learns of his deception and drops him like the proverbial "hot potato." She drops him not because he did not meet up to her standards (he is sensitive, romantic, and thoroughly endearing), but because he unintentionally hurt her with his deception. The truth of the matter is that had he introduced her to his real personality, he would have won her over to him.

Just a movie? Perhaps. Yet it happens frequently. A case in point:

I was in L.A. with a business associate for a commercial shooting. We stayed at the Beverly Hills Hotel, which is also a hangout for aspiring young starlets who hope to meet a famous actor, director, or producer capable of contributing to their future success. My business associate got the bright idea to have himself paged at the bar for an alleged phone conversation with an important producer in full view and earshot of these gorgeous, job-hungry starlets. The outcome was predictable. As soon as he finished his contrived conversation, the women jockeyed into position to get close to him. He had the pick of the group. Unfortunately for him, one of the women whom he was leading on discovered he was a fraud and created a truly ugly scene. My business associate was profoundly embarrassed—but he deserved it!

So accept yourself for who and what you are. Let the real you come through in your encounters and the relationships you establish will be lasting.

DON'T INTERROGATE

"Hold it!" you say. "On one hand you say, 'Ask questions' and on the other you say, 'Don't interrogate.' This is confusing. This is contradictory. This is getting complicated!"

Well, let me see if we can clarify this a bit. You should ask questions, but it's the way you ask those questions that is important. I'm sure you'll agree that a given collection of words can carry different meanings by simply changing the inflection and/or tone of your voice. In addition, the way you ask questions, the type of questions, the rapidity of questioning, and your tone of voice makes for varying impressions. Here are a few easy rules of thumb:

- *Don't probe!* You're not the district attorney prosecuting a case. Nobody likes being grilled.
- *Take your time.* You don't need to direct questions in rapid fire at others. Give women an opportunity to answer your questions. Listen to what they're telling you.

- *Exchange information.* Don't attempt to get personal. Tell the woman with whom you're speaking why you are interested in her answers.
- *Make your questions invitations to discussion.* Keep away from close-ended questions that can be answered with a single word response.

DON'T HOLD BACK YOUR FEELINGS

Let your interest in women radiate. Open up with some important information about yourself, and you'll find she will do the same. There's no easier way to tear down the defenses of today's woman than by letting her see the real you. The reason for this is that by allowing your true feelings to come through you gain her trust and confidence.

ONE MORE DON'T

Don't let this listing get you down. Think about the positive suggestions inherent in each and every one of these rules of the road. They'll help your prospects for developing a relationship with today's woman following a third party introduction. In short, have confidence in your ability to establish productive relationships. Listen carefully to what women are telling you with their words and actions. Demonstrate your interest in others with questions that will promote conversations. Direct the conversation away from controversial subjects. Let the real you shine forth in all your encounters. Exchange information about yourself. Above all, stay loose and enjoy yourself!

CHAPTER FIVE

HOW TO BREAK THE ICE WITH A COMPLETE (BUT BEAUTIFUL) STRANGER

You step into the elevator on the twenty-third floor and push the button on the control console marked "L" for lobby. In the isolation of the elevator, you begin wrestling with the idea of renting a beach house for the summer with a couple of your buddies. Scenes of the parties, the surf, good food and times, and the lovely women whose company will grace the beach house flash into your mind.

Suddenly, the elevator stops at the twentieth floor, the doors open, and in steps the woman of your dreams. She's petite. She's demure. She appears well-bred. What's more she's gorgeous. As the doors close and the elevator begins its descent you find yourself caught short of breath by her beauty. Her blonde hair looks as soft and rich as silk, cascading down to her bare, delicate shoulders. Her large eyes shine a bright blue, clear as a fast-running stream. Each feature of her face appears sharply chiseled by a master craftsman. And her lips are full-bodied and inviting. Her figure is well proportioned with each curve beckoning for your touch.

You feel as though the elevator is racing, plummeting madly down toward the lobby. And as you hurtle down past each floor you feel your stomach and heart rushing up into your head. Soon you can hear nothing but your heart beating in your ears...faster...

louder... faster.... Your mouth becomes dry and your hands go clammy with anticipation. Your eyes dance wildly to behold her beauty as if captured by the splendor of untamed flames reaching upward toward the stars. If you could only reach over to the control console to freeze your fast fleeting moments with her. If only there was some way to meet her. If only someone you knew would climb aboard the elevator before it reached the lobby and say, "John, I'd like you to meet Claire. She just rented an apartment in our building."

The elevator comes to an abrupt halt and your eyes dart to the display board where much to your dismay you see the letter "L" brightly illuminated. The doors open and a force immobilizes you against the back panel as she walks out before you. After what passes as an eternity you begin to follow behind, caught in a hypnotic state by the gentle swaying of her hips. It's almost like a dream. Everything is blotted out but the magnificence of her grace, and you hear nothing but the sound of your heart beating. You begin to panic with the realization that this dream will end and with it she will step out of your life—forever.

A taxi stops at the curb, and you watch her get in it. She smiles out to you as she exposes her long, slender gams before your eyes. Then the taxi speeds out of sight, and she's out of your life.

Every day for the next week you ride the elevator up and down from the twenty-third floor, hoping that you will see her once again. However, you don't see her. Perhaps she was just visiting a friend. Perhaps she was inquiring about an apartment for rent. It doesn't matter because you know you'll never see her again. You'll never know the touch of her lips, the feel of her hair, the sound of her voice, the pleasure of her company.

You could have spoken with her. You know how to converse with women. But you lacked one important input—a third party introduction. So what do you do when you meet the woman of your dreams and you don't have the advantage of a third party introduction? Simple, *you introduce yourself.*

THE INTRODUCTION

Let's replay the scene. Suddenly, the elevator stops at the twentieth floor and in steps the woman of your dreams. You give her a broad smile and warm, "Hello."

She returns your smile and greets you with an energetic, "Hi."

YOU: "I'm afraid we haven't met. My name is ..." You reach out your hand for hers.

SHE: "I'm Claire." She takes your outstretched hand.

YOU: "I'm pleased to meet you Claire. Claire are you new here?"

SHE: "Well not quite yet. I just finished looking over an apartment for rent on the twentieth floor. I really like it, but I'm not sure I'll take it."

YOU: "Claire, I've been living here for about three years now. Perhaps I can tell you more about the neighborhood and neighbors. If you have a few minutes, let's stop by the coffee shop and I'll fill you in."

SHE: "Thanks. I'd really like that."

Voilà! You made your own introduction, and with it went the deed on a potential new relationship. Admittedly, it took a wee bit more courage and ingenuity. Yet, you have everything it takes to make your own introduction. You know that if you're going to expand your circle of intimate friends this is the way it generally happens. The truth of the matter is that there's not a mutual friend tucked away behind the bushes to pop out and introduce you to the beautiful stranger you see on the street, at the library, bus station, grocery store, or skating rink. Instead, it's up to you to introduce yourself and establish contact.

BREAKING THE ICE

Here are a few effective ways in which you can break the ice with a complete stranger:

CURRENT ENVIRONMENT: Picture this. You're seated next to a very attractive woman on the "red-eye special" from Los Angeles to New York, and you want to make contact with her. What can you do? For openers talk about the current environment—the flight, the weather conditions, the service, food, and beverages. You can move on easily from your opening remarks. When the conversation begins to slow down, explore other topics such as the book she's reading, her hometown, the nature of her trip, and basic background data.

The opportunity to make contact with this approach is available in just about any environment or situation. It makes little difference whether you're on a late-night flight or 5:30 p.m. commuter run on your local railroad. For that matter, the opportunity is just as available at a party, sporting event, concert, in a subway, or wherever people gather. The current environment provides you with a tailor-made opportunity to make contact. Simply talk about the surrounding facilities, personalities, furnishings, dress, people you've met, and ambiance, and the possibilities are all laid out before you. They're limited by nothing but your own powers of imagination, observation, and willingness to make contact.

ASK FOR HELP OR INFORMATION: This approach capitalizes on the need of others to feel important and to be of service. Questions such as, "Can you tell me where you bought that handsome attache case?" or, "How do I get to Bleeker Street?" or, "Where can I find a good Chinese restaurant that's not too expensive?" They are all effective ways in which you can establish that initial contact.

Corny? Perhaps it is. But it is still a popular and valuable approach. Besides, although originality is of value, there's no reason to believe that the "tried and true" methods won't work for you. If you're hung up on being original perhaps you can try a whimsical approach. Ask for something out of the ordinary, such as, "Could you tell me in which of these homes George Washington slept?"

Your contact will be well aware that you're not serious about needing help or information but should come away flattered that you find her sufficiently attractive to make contact.

CHIVALRY: Not chauvinism, chivalry. There's a real distinction between the two. In employing chivalry you're really displaying social grace and a caring attitude. In today's macho society, where the attitude belies a put-down of women, chivalry is refreshing, pleasing, and genuinely welcome.

If you're on that "red-eye special" from L.A. to New York, you might offer to get her a pillow while you're up. Or perhaps you could stow her coat away in the overhead compartment. Or you could place her carry-on luggage beneath her seat. If you're commuting on the railroad, bus, or subway it would be gallant to offer her your seat. You could help her carry her grocery bags from the store to her car or hold a door open while she passes through. All of these chivalrous acts serve as icebreakers in which you can go on to introduce yourself to a complete stranger.

WIT AND HUMOR: You're sitting in the lobby of your dentist's office, awaiting your turn. Across from you is a lovely woman. She looks interesting and available (no ring). So you decide you're going to make a play for her. But alas, this is a dog-eat-dog world. To her right sits another young man. He's handsome, well-groomed and nattily dressed. What's more he's a real wit. He starts talking to her about the current environment before you can draw back your lips. She laughs with him. In fact, he's so funny he has the receptionist, the dental hygienist, your dentist, and his patient all laughing. Now everybody is laughing, including you. This guy's wit has won him the name and number of not only the woman across from you, but the receptionist and hygienist as well. What's more the dentist is going to examine him before you, and you're not even perturbed because he is funny, a keen wit, one whom everyone wishes to be like.

Fantasy? Sure. Nevertheless, there's more truth to it than one cares to admit. The wit, the individual with the quick humor or funny anecdote is a hero's model for movies, plays, songs, and books. We all enjoy a good laugh, and most of us envy those with the talent to draw a crowd and make them laugh. The fact is that most people are not capable of being comedians. More importantly, not all people share the same sense of humor. In other words, what you may consider sidesplitting could fail to draw a smile from another.

Nonetheless, the use of humor can be an effective icebreaker, one you may want to try. If you do, consider the following:

- *Keep it clean.* The late Lenny Bruce may have been able to get away with the ribald and obscene, but you'll find few people who are attuned to vulgarity, particularly from a stranger.
- *Keep it natural.* Contrived humor often falls short. Specifically, not everyone shares the same sense of humor, and most of us don't have the penchant for telling jokes in true comedic fashion. Let your humor flow from the environment or situation. It's something you can both share.
- *Keep it short.* Although nothing is harder to do, it's better to bow out while you're still hot. Wrap it up before others grow bored and move on to more stimulating conversation.
- *If you're going to tell a joke make sure you know it well.* I've seen many a soul who has captured the ears of a small audience lose them because he failed to get the punch line or sequence of the joke right. If you like to tell jokes, it might be a good idea to jot down the jokes you like best and review them occasionally to keep them fresh in your mind.

THE DIRECT APPROACH: This approach clearly represents a form of flattery. It says to the woman being approached that you believe she is interesting, attractive, and a worthwhile person. She's so worthwhile, in fact, that you want to get to know her. The direct approach works something like this, "Hi, my name is Pete. Excuse me for being so forward but I couldn't help but notice you among all these people. So I just had to learn more about you. What's your name?"

More than likely she'll proceed to tell you her name and graciously thank you for the compliment. She might even ask you to clarify and expand upon what it is that you believe sets her apart from the others present. When she does this, you've a firm foothold on establishing a productive contact—one that you may cultivate into a full blown, intimate relationship.

One of the most famous examples of the power of the direct approach originated in the days when this continent was first settled by the Pilgrims. If I remember my history correctly, Miles Standish was in love with a young maiden named Priscilla Alden. So was John Smith. Yet, because of his respect for Mr. Standish, John allowed himself to be the go-between for Miles—to profess Miles' love for Priscilla and ask for her hand in marriage. Priscilla was in love also, but with John, not Miles. When John approached Priscilla on behalf of Miles, she replied, "John speak for yourself." And Priscilla Alden scored with a direct approach.

Many shy from this approach at first for fear of rejection (as did Miles). It takes more than the average quota of courage to' make contact with this approach because you lay your feelings on the line. However, don't let that discourage you from taking the dirrect approach. It is extremely effective in making a productive contact. This approach releases the real you in the mix. It conveys what you feel and think of others in a truly flattering and complimentary manner. Try it.

THE COMPLIMENT: The compliment satisfies the needs of others to feel important, to be recognized, accepted, and liked. However, there is one key ingredient. Your compliments must be for real. You must be genuine or people will see through you. Instead of making others feel important, they'll feel insulted. You don't get close by insulting people.

It's easy to pay others genuine compliments. There's always that something special that attracted your attention in the first place.

All you need to do is acknowledge that positive attribute. It could be her smile, her eyes, the way she wears her hair, her femininity, the sound of her voice, her taste in clothes, or her jewelry. As you can see, there are many possibilities.

Additionally, there are indirect ways in which you can compliment people. When someone provides you with an interesting perspective you hadn't considered, tell her. If someone tells you or does something interesting, tell her that also. These are equally as effective in letting others know you think they're special.

THE CASE OF MISTAKEN IDENTITY: There are two variations to this approach. The first is not all that flattering, and so I suggest you shy away from it. I present it only to make you aware of it and its potential consequences. Basically, it goes something like this, "Don't I know you from somewhere?" My feeling is that if the individual is worth remembering you wouldn't have forgotten if, when, and where you met her.

The second approach can be productive. You comment that your encounter reminds you of someone you know, such as a sister, cousin, or close friend. This provides you with an opportunity to compliment or talk further about the characteristic or attribute that reminds you of another. I wouldn't suggest that you use this approach either unless it is sincere. Many people may have the impression that you're "feeding them a line."

In summary, when the girl of your dreams materializes, take it upon yourself to make the introduction. Approach her in a confident manner. Use any one or a combination of the approaches suggested here. And don't be afraid to use your own ingenuity. Play the situation as you see it. Keep alert to the feedback you receive and modify your approach accordingly to keep the conversation flowing. Your potential for bringing about new relationships will increase multifold by your new knowledge and willingness to break the ice with desirable strangers.

CHAPTER SIX

THREE WINNING TECHNIQUES FOR BREAKING A WOMAN'S RESISTANCE

Unfortunately, women often unknowingly build barriers during their initial encounters with others. These barriers create distance and stand in the way of a free exchange of feelings between a man and woman. They result from the fear that they will not be perceived favorably, and they generally will not come down until mutual trust is established. Unless these barriers are lifted the encounter will probably not progress beyond the small talk stage.

Here are three winning techniques that can help you tear down the barriers and melt the distance that women may unwittingly create. They can help you develop the trust needed to break a woman's resistance and provide the foundation for achieving intimacy.

THE POWER OF TOUCHING

Picture this: It's Sunday morning. You turn on the TV and on the screen you see a man of the cloth—an imposing figure—imploring some suffering member of his congregation to come forward and be healed. Out of the audience appears an elderly woman who drags herself forward with the aid of two crutches. Your heart goes out to her. She's at least seventy. She approaches slowly and cautiously, crippled by some malady that has left one of her legs atrophied.

She gets down on one knee before him. The preacher asks for God's help as he places his hands gently upon her head. He asks the woman to believe and be healed. He urges the congregation to join him in prayer so that this woman may be healed, all the while pressing his hands gently upon her head.

The old woman feels his touch. It's strong but gentle. Warm. Caring. Confident. Through his touch she feels a greater force that passes into her body, her spirit, and into her withered stick of a leg. Lo and behold, before hundreds of thousands of viewers, she picks herself up and walks off without the aid of her crutches. The entire congregation cries with joy at the apparent miracle they've witnessed. A miracle affected by the touch of a mere mortal's hands. And you wonder if it's for real.

A great deal of research has been conducted that proves the power of touching. These studies show that touching is an effective tool in relieving stress, and comforting and even healing psychic pain. Yes, touching is a powerful force, and it can be used to break the resistance of women, making acquaintances of strangers, friends of acquaintances, and lovers of friends. Touching adds extra dimension to words. It conveys fondness, admiration, affection, gentleness, thoughtfulness, concern, ease with others, and a basic warmth—all of which serve to overcome any lack of trust.

UNLEASH THE POWER OF TOUCHING

Touching is an important need that each of us share. Unfortunately, most people restrain the urge to reach out and share their true feelings with others. The reason for restraint is largely cultural. Unlike most Americans, many of the people from other societies freely engage in touching during their conversations. An additional reason for restraint is that many of us are afraid that others may mistake our sign for affection or fondness as a sexual advance. Worse yet, many of us are afraid of being rebuffed for taking the liberty of closing in on another's personal space.

Touching is such an important urge and powerful tool that we need to overcome any inhibitions and reach out to others. Touching is one of the most powerful techniques to break the resistance of women and get closer to them. In fact, your touch can be one of the more lasting and compelling impressions women get of you. So reach out and touch today's woman in a profound sense through physical contact. Here are a few suggestions.

During the initial phases of your encounter, time your touches carefully to avoid any mistaken impression of a sexual advance. Some of the ways you might touch include, but are not limited to offering your arm to a woman as you guide her up to the bar for a drink or touching her arm as you share a laugh over a funny anecdote. Also, try to integrate your touches with nonverbal communication to put others at ease.

If you really feel constrained, touch some inanimate object. For example, you might transfer your touch to a watch, bracelet, or ring as you admire its beauty. This will help break the ice and pave the way for more intimate expressions of physical contact.

SMILE

It's incredible what a smile can do for your looks. When you smile you look your best. There are no two ways about it. The other day I came across a magazine ad that illustrated this point. It was an ad for a shampoo that is supposed to make your hair look and feel less greasy. It displayed side by side photographs of a woman both "before" (with greasy, stringy hair) and "after" (with magnificent, full-bodied hair) using the shampoo. The thing that really struck me though, was her smile. I covered her hair in each of the photos to study her face. In the "before" photo she wore a look of concern, anxiety, and consternation. On the other hand, the "after" photo captured a winning smile that radiated the model's beauty. Her eyes appeared so much brighter, her facial expression more animated, and she came off looking younger, more exuberant, vital, and inviting.

When you smile, you're more than just a pretty face. An honest-to-goodness smile can melt the distance between others. It conveys a basic warmth and beauty that comes from deep inside of you where it truly counts. Importantly, a genuine smile will serve to put women at ease, opening them up to both you and a potential new relationship. Your smile is intoxicating and will help today's woman forget her anxieties. Such is the beauty of your smile.

THE SWEET SOUND OF THY NAME

One of the most powerful words in the English language is the sound of our own name. It resonates in the air and shatters the walls between people. Using another's name throughout a conversation helps to establish a tone of familiarity. Psychologically, I believe it makes people feel as though they're old friends, as opposed to two strangers meeting for the first time. This apparent familiarity helps establish mutual trust and admiration. Furthermore, use of another's name keeps you "other directed." As such, women will feel more important, appreciated, and respected. We know from previous discussions that the best way to get women interested in you is to be "other directed."

In summary, touching, smiling and the liberal mention of another's name will help tear down the barriers and melt the distance between you and the women you meet. Each can help you turn complete strangers into friends and, perhaps, lovers.

CHAPTER SEVEN

WHERE TO FIND WOMEN WHO ARE OPEN TO INTIMATE NEW RELATIONSHIPS

Cat Stevens popularized the words from the song, "Another Saturday Night" by Sam Cooke. It's about a poor soul with money and time on his hands who is looking for a woman to help him enjoy it. Unfortunately, he can't seem to "meet 'em." Which brings up an important question: "Where do you find desirable, available women who are open to new relationships with you?"

The answer: *everywhere*. In fact, the more appropriate question is: "Where *can't* you find desirable, available women who are open to new relationships with you?"

LOOK WHEREVER PEOPLE ARE

Potential contacts are available wherever people are. We need to change our thinking that there are "designated" places for new contacts and the possibility of meeting women is limited to those "designated" places. We can make contact with the woman sitting next to us on the subway, or the woman on line at the checkout counter in the grocery store, or the woman sitting at the next table in the restaurant. Certainly some places may offer more opportunities than others. After all, people go to a singles' bar for the express purpose of meeting others, but there's the potential to make contact anywhere you find other people.

There is one exception. You won't meet women sitting home in front of the "boob tube" or reading the sports page. You have to make the effort to get out of your home or apartment to meet women. If you adopt the attitude that you're interested in meeting new women to share a relationship you won't pass up the opportunities that exist and are available to you every day.

Here are some places that offer better than average potential for meeting desirable, available women who are open to new relationships with you. Additionally, I've listed a few icebreakers that have proven particularly effective in these situations.

NIGHT SCHOOLS

Today's woman is interested in bettering herself. She's either working to land a new or better job or to cultivate new interests. The women enrolled in night schools are particularly interesting because of their ambition, energy level, and interests. Moreover, night school is somewhat like a social club. The people attending share common interests, and take pride in their membership and the sacrifices they are making to keep up with their work. So, if you want to meet interesting women consider finishing the college work you started or enroll for a master's degree. Or, just enroll in an adult education course and take up something you're interested in learning. A few years ago I became interested in learning how to play the guitar and enrolled in a beginners' class offered as part of the adult education curriculum in a local high school. I met women who shared my interest in music and learning how to play the guitar. As a result of that class (and subsequent guitar classes), I developed some lasting relationships.

ICEBREAKERS YOU CAN USE AT SCHOOL

- "Excuse me, but could you please tell me where I can find room No. 326?" This is the *Asking For Help* approach. Then you can go on to tell her that you're new to the school. You can ask her how long she's been enrolled, what she's studying, and so forth.

- "I like the way you play that tune. You have a fine sense of timing and really know how to make the music come to life." A *Compliment* spoken to one who is in your music class. Obviously, you have an opportunity to pay a compliment in any crafts oriented class.
- "Hi, my name is Dave. I couldn't help but notice you, and well, I just wanted to introduce myself." Here is the *Direct Approach*. Deliver it with enthusiasm and warmth.
- "Could you tell me where you bought that book bag? It looks both smart and functional." *Ask For Information* and give a *Compliment*.
- "I've heard Mr. Dent is a fantastic teacher. He makes everything so easy and interesting. What have you heard about him?" The *Current Environment* approach. If she knows something, you can exchange information. If she doesn't you can go on to tell her more.

TRANSPORTATION

Whether it be a bus, subway, commuter railroad, ferry, or airplane, you have a good opportunity to make contacts. The key is to use the opportunity. For example, sit yourself (where possible) next to someone you feel you would be interested in meeting. Or, walk along the bus stop or train terminal and position yourself next to those women you find appealing.

MOBILE ICEBREAKERS

- "Here, let me put that bag up" (as you reach out to grab her bag). "That looks pretty heavy to me." *Chivalry*.
- "Hmmm. I do believe they have the air conditioning running today. That means it's probably going to snow." *Humor*. It's 90 degrees outside, but the railroad's air conditioning hasn't been all that reliable in the past. Believe me, this is a humorous approach. Admittedly, it is wry humor for those people who suffer through riding the uncomfortable and unpredictable railroad everyday.
- "What's that your reading? The reason I ask is I enjoy reading and I'm always in the market for another good book." *Asking For Information*. Most importantly, you probably share a mutual interest.
- "I hope you don't think I'm too forward, but I notice you take this train everyday, and I just wanted to sit next to you so I could meet

you. I'm Bill Williams and I work for RCA. What's your name and what do you do?" *Direct Approach.*

- "Excuse me, but why don't you take my seat." *Chivalry* on a crowded bus.

SINGLES' BARS

Why do you think women go to a singles' bar? They go to meet men like you. So you really don't need to beat around the bush. On the other hand, remember that you do want and should strive to make the women you meet feel that they're special, unique, interesting, and truly desirable—not like they are just another conquest.

SINGLES' OPENERS

- "Hi, I'm Tim Peterson." State your name with energy, and wear a broad and sincere smile. "What's yours?" *Direct Approach.* Go on to tell her why, among all the people present you wanted to meet her.
- "You look like you're ready for a refill. Let me buy you a drink. I'm Bill Randolph." Again, state your name with energy and wear a broad and sincere smile. *Direct Approach.*
- "Would you be interested in meeting a warm, personable, charming young man who also happens to be wealthy, debonair, a celebrity among jet setters, and a master brain surgeon?" ("Yes," she says.) "Well, then how about someone who is just a warm, personable, charming young man?" (Said with a broad smile.) *Humor.*

VACATION SPOTS

Plan your vacation wisely. Get out for a change. Not just to the local beach, although it is a prime area for meeting women. You can make that trip anytime. Instead, use your time to visit some area you've never been to before. Take in sunny California or ride up to Bar Harbour, Maine. How about a cruise to Nassau or the Bahamas? You won't be alone. There will be plenty of women who are out for a good time, to take in new sights, and to meet new people. The relationships you make on vacation can be intimate and lasting. It could very well be a result of just being away from the grind at the office or the fact that everyone is looking for a good time. Whatever the reasons, you'll find vacation spots and hideaways are prime areas to meet interesting new people.

ICEBREAKERS ABROAD

- "Wow, that sun!" Shout it with exuberance as you lie spreadeagle on your blanket. "We just don't have sun like this in New York City. What about you?" *Current Environment.*
- "You look like you're getting pretty burned from the sun. Would you care for some tanning lotion?" *Chivalry.*
- "You look like a woman of exceptional good taste. Could you fill me in on some of the better places to eat and interesting sights to take in?" *Asking For Help And Information.*
- "Hold it. Don't move. I'd like to snap your picture to show my friends back home some of the really beautiful sights!" *Compliment* with a creative touch.

SHOPPING MALLS AND CENTERS

These provide you with an opportunity to shop for some new contacts—at little cost to you. Buying and window shopping serves as a form of amusement for many of us. Walk into a shopping center on a Thursday night or Saturday morning, and you'll generally find it teeming with women. More importantly, you can find women who share the same interests as you by frequenting stores that cater to your interests (record shop if you're into music; the book store if you enjoy reading). You also could make contact with many a desirable and available clerk and saleswoman.

SHOPPING FOR CONTACTS

- "What do you know about this book?" You *Ask For Information* from a woman who is leafing through a book in your vicinity.

- "Excuse me, but I'm stuck. I'm shopping for a birthday present for my sister, and well, I like your taste in dress. Perhaps if you're not in a hurry, you could take a few minutes and give me some ideas for her." *Asking For Help* and *Compliment.* This is a hard one to resist since most people enjoy shopping, and you're making this person feel very important with your compliment and request.
- "Hi, I'm Ron Eagan. I don't introduce myself to strangers, but I think you're gorgeous and wanted to meet you." *Direct Approach* with *Compliment.*
- "That's a beautiful bracelet you're wearing. Is it a family heirloom?" *Compliment* to saleswoman.
- "I must tell you, you're not only lovely but extremely courteous, and efficient. I don't know how you do it, but I'd like to compliment you to your boss." *Compliment.*

SINGLES' CLUBS

Singles' clubs are springing up in nearly every community. There are clubs for singles over 30, for divorced men and women, for people of all ages. Many of them are affiliated with local community centers and churches. They provide an ideal opportunity for you to meet women who are also interested in establishing new relationships. So, like the singles' bars, you don't need to waste time. Check your local newspaper, church bulletin, or adult education center for the availability of these clubs in your area.

SEARCHING OUT SINGLES

Here are a few suggested ways you might break the ice:

- "May I have this dance?" *Direct Approach.* Most of these clubs stage dances on a regular basis. And, unless already committed, most women won't refuse an invitation.
- "Hi, I'm Ken Johnston. I couldn't help but notice you from among everyone here tonight. I think it's your eyes, they're so expressive." *Direct Approach* with *Compliment.*
- "Hi, isn't it super that the community sponsors events such as this. It really gives singles an opportunity to meet people with similar

interests. I'm Jim Raines. Who are you?" *Current Environment* with *Direct Approach.*

ATHLETIC ASSOCIATIONS/CLUBS

As discussed earlier, the "Me generation" is interested in their own physical well-being and related activities. They're affiliated with the local runners' club, exercise regularly at the health spas, or hold memberships at tennis and racquetball centers. They're into clubs and associations not just for the exercise, but also because they truly enjoy the activities. If you have an interest in tennis, running, backpacking, or whatever, look into becoming affiliated with a club or association in your area. You won't have any problems breaking the ice with the women present because they'll either introduce themselves ("Hi, and welcome to the club!") or you'll find tailor-made activities such as tennis matches.

OTHER OPPORTUNITIES

Other popular places include but are not limited to:

GROCERY STORE: This is a good spot for you to meet women. The ratio of women to men is extremely high. Asking for help is a particularly effective way to break the ice in the grocery store. You can easily ask advice regarding the selection of meats, best way to cook a roast, use of spices, and so forth.

BEACH: Women flock to the beaches as soon as the warm weather approaches to enjoy the surf, the sun's rays, and to just plain relax. The beach or poolside is a good place to meet women. You already share one interest—beach activities. You might ask for or offer help in applying suntan lotion, try a direct approach, compliment, or try your own creative way!

CHURCH: Many churches offer more than spiritual renewal. They appreciate and respect the needs of their congregation and provide ample opportunity through planned socials to share fellowship. Check into the churches in your area to learn what they can offer you.

AND STILL MORE PLACES!

If you still think it's difficult to meet the woman of your dreams consider the following places where you can "find 'em":

Movies	Laundromats
Theatre	Ice Skating or Roller Rinks
Library	Elevators
Charity Functions	Places of Employment
Dances	Basketball Games
Discos	Ski Resorts
Museums	Town Meetings
Zoo	Drama Clubs
State Fairs	Amusement Parks
Restaurants	Volunteer Groups

I think you'll agree there are virtually no limits to places where you can "meet 'em." It could be on an elevator ride up to your office or a cruise to the Bahamas. The key is to keep alert to new opportunities and seize them when they come available.

CHAPTER EIGHT

HOW TO READ A WOMAN LIKE A BOOK

I had an interesting experience at an introductory sales seminar that is definitely important in understanding women. The presenter was attempting to sell his course of sales instruction to various government agencies, business enterprises, and organizations that employ some form of personal selling to achieve their objectives.

I literally hung on every word the presenter said in an attempt to pick up his sales techniques and evaluate his sales skills. Interestingly, only twenty minutes into his presentation he stopped speaking, walked to the back of the auditorium, addressed one of the attendees, and signed that man's organization up for the complete course in sales instruction. Needless to say, I was quite amazed and suitably impressed at what I had seen transpire. The presenter, only part way through his introductory sales demonstration, was able to identify an interested party out of the throng of attendees. Then, right before us all, he stopped his presentation to close the sale he knew he had made.

I asked him how he knew his prospect was ready to buy. I really had to know this "outstanding" technique for identifying his prospect's interest, particularly since that prospect hadn't uttered a single word. The presenter responded that words weren't necessary because he could gauge a prospect's interest, or the lack thereof, by the way a prospect carried himself, sat, by his facial expressions, and his general countenance. In other words, the presenter understood what Julius Fast and others have recently popularized as body language, body talk, or nonverbal communications.

The presenter related his account of what had happened. As he took the podium, he couldn't help but be struck by the appearance of a very uptight, defensive prospect sitting near an exit who was ready to tune out the presentation given any reasonable, or for that matter, unreasonable, excuse. The presenter pointed out that the signs of this man's defensiveness and lack of interest were fairly obvious. The man sat deep within his chair, arms crossed with his hands balled tightly into fists, jacket buttoned, head thrown back as if "turning his nose up" to the presenter, jaws clamped shut, brows furrowed, and mouth set into a grimace. Additionally, the prospect's legs were crossed (facing the exit) and he kicked his foot up and down impatiently. The presenter immediately judged from all this, based on previous experience, that before him sat a rather defensive individual who had probably been directed by a superior to attend the seminar against his best interest and protestations.

The presenter took off his jacket, loosened his tie, smiled, and warmly addressed the group, being careful to make eye contact with the audience and expose the palms of his hands. As he continued talking, he related his products to the needs of the individuals in attendance. He began to witness a thawing in the defensive man's posture. The prospect uncrossed his legs, planting them firmly on the floor. He unlocked his arms and fists, and brought an opened hand to the side of his face. His gaze steadied on the presenter, and his head tilted to the side as though he were intently evaluating every word the presenter said.

As the presenter went on to relate concrete examples of how the skills acquired in his sales instruction course were used to dramatically improve on the sales of individuals and organizations, he observed a complete reversal in the man's attitude. The prospect leaned forward in his seat, jacket opened, and hand placed on his thigh. His eyes opened wide as if in anticipation, and his mouth broke into a broad smile as he nodded affirmatively at the presenter's examples. It was at that moment, the presenter stated, that he knew he had made a sale.

This presenter was able to make a very profitable sale, which as you might imagine led to several others, by interpreting the body language of a prospect. You, too, can use a better understanding of body language to identify women who are open to new relationships; to gain feedback about whether you're being accepted by them; to spark added confidence; and to open up today's woman to you, stimulating added responsiveness.

THE BODY'S LANGUAGE

Body language is certainly not new. It is a term coined for the speech of kinesics, which is the study of body gestures, movements, and motions as they relate to speech. In fact, body language is thought to account for much of the contact and communications that goes on between people.

As mentioned before, women are particularly adept at interpreting and employing body language. However, we all understand body gestures and interpret body movements and motions to varying degrees. How often have you "sensed" that your relationship with another person was somewhat amiss? Or, how often have you picked up what you felt were good "vibes" from new acquaintances? Your "nose for sensing" and the so-called "vibes" you picked up may be attributed to your ability to read body gestures. These gestures are not just a single body movement but a series of motions that paint a rather clear picture of general responsiveness. My presenter friend, as you'll recall, was able to piece together many individual body expressions into *coherent groupings* that allowed him to accurately assess his prospect's general attitudes, feelings, and responsiveness. With added awareness of the significance of body gestures and practice, you can become conversant in body language as well. You'll be able to more clearly assess behavioral interaction and increase the likelihood of establishing meaningful, intimate relationships with women.

HOW TO READ
A WOMAN'S INTEREST IN YOU

We're all interested, first and foremost, in whether others are truly interested in us. We hunger for genuine signs of approval, acceptance, liking, and interest. So, it is only natural that we start with a review of body gestures that express interest.

PREENING—GET READY: Preening gestures will generally be evidenced in instances where interest in a member of the opposite sex exists. Preening can be body gestures that attempt to improve one's appearance in order to create a favorable physical impression on others. Preening gestures may be manifested as attempts at "freshening up" to look one's best. You're probably familiar with many of these gestures because you've either consciously or unconsciously preened for someone you admired.

A change in posture and body carriage often are signs of preening. A man might throw his shoulders back and expand his chest. At the same time he might stand erect to enhance his physical stature. He'll suck in his stomach and draw his muscles taut to fully display his masculinity. Furthermore, he'll take added pains to carefully arrange his clothes—ensure his tie is straight, shirt is tucked in, pants and jacket are lint-free, and so on. In today's society you might catch him smoothing a mustache, beard, and full mane of hair.

A woman's gestures are very similar. The differences that exist between men and women in preening reflect natural differences in sex. She, too, will throw back her shoulders and thrust out her breasts to prominently display that which is most affectatious to many men. She'll stand tall and pull in her stomach to enhance the provocativeness of her figure. And, like the man, she will smooth her clothes and perhaps rearrange any jewelry she's wearing. Naturally, there is the arranging of hair as well—she might brush it back away from her forehead, tuck it behind her ear and/or delicately balance it at the back of her head.

TELLTALE SIGNS   But women go well beyond preening to consciously or subconsciously signify interest. One such movement that has been exploited in movies to connote "sexual" interest is the seductive use of the tongue in touching the lips. The meaning of this gesture has been overdone in both the cinema and popular novels. It's fair to assume that touching the lips with the tongue evidences interest, but it's a bit much to assume that this signifies the woman is eager to have sexual relations.

Another movement that may be employed by women to signify interest is the revealing of their thighs via the careful crossing and uncrossing of the legs. This gesture, like the use of the tongue to touch the lips, has been overdone in film and print to signify more than a casual interest. An interested woman might also tuck a leg under her as she sits and converses. Give yourself extra points if she sits facing you, is highly animated, fixes her eyes on you, and wears a bright smile. Obviously, the latter body movements are not limited to the feminine gender.

Still another is the balancing of the woman's shoe on her toes. As you might imagine, this probably shows that she is relaxed in your presence. The "batting of the eyes," rapid blinking of the eyelids as the eyes move freely about, might also be favorably registered (unless the "Southern Belle" happens to bat her eyes at everyone with whom she tends to come into contact). And, we can't overlook the feminine gesture that every man welcomes when he enters a disco, party, bar, or whatever in the hopes of making a new contact—the sideways glance coupled with a tailor-made smile. If she should turn her head away, don't be concerned. Our society dictates just so much "looking" between strangers. Nevertheless, the smile is your invitation to become better acquainted.

TOUCHING IS TELLING: Touching is a body gesture employed by both sexes. It can be used to show affection, as a signal to speak, and to reassure. Whatever the specific reason, touching indicates active involvement, and in my book, that spells interest! Touching is a very personal, warm way of displaying interest. Unfortunately, in our culture touching isn't all that commonplace.

In fact, the first touch between new acquaintances is often the "accidental brush," as opposed to body contact in the traditional sense. On the other hand, there are the "touchers", who by their very nature are generous in displaying their interest via a touch of an arm and hand. Should you come into contact with this type of endearing action, reciprocate. You will further that woman's interest in you.

The manner in which a woman uses her arms and hands can indicate openness and receptivity. The gesture to keep an eye out for is open hands (dread the fist) with frequent showing of the palms. Consider for a moment many of the paintings and sculptures of Christ, who is often depicted with arms open and palms showing. This is symbolic for openness and sincerity. Coupled with the unrestrained, fluid use of the arms, palms showing often bespeaks a woman who is relaxed and, perhaps, confident in your presence.

KEEP YOUR DISTANCE: The amount of physical distance a new acquaintance establishes between you and her can be an indicator of her interest in you. In other cultures it may be perfectly acceptable to stand and speak, literally, face to face. However, consider your reaction to someone you just met if he were to position himself just inches from you. In our culture you keep your distance, and make sure you don't invade anyone else's personal space. On the other hand, you probably wouldn't mind—as a matter of fact, I'm sure you'd welcome—having your personal space infringed on by an alluring beauty whose company and conversation you had been enjoying. Now, if she were to step within your space after having smothered you with warm, spontaneous smiles, generous touching, and deep gazes, you'd be more than justified to accept this as a sign of genuine interest.

Another positive body gesture is nodding. When she nods as you speak, she is saying that she hears what you're saying, understands you, wants you to continue speaking, and may even agree with you. As such, the nod is a very encouraging gesture.

Not to overlook the obvious, let's not forget the smile or direct eye contact. There are many different types of smiles, each smile carrying a special meaning when accompanied by supplementary or complementary body gestures. There are two types of smiles, however, that express degrees of positive involvement. There is what is referred to as the upper smile, which exposes the upper teeth only. This smile is often accompanied by direct eye contact and is frequently used to greet others. Then, there's the broad, toothy smile revealing both upper and lower teeth. As contrasted to the upper smile, this is generally accompanied by less direct eye contact. In fact, the head might be thrown back, exposing the neck. The difference between the two smiles reflects degree of involvement. While the upper smile may represent acknowledgment, the broad smile connotes deeper involvement, the type of involvement associated with laughing.

Not all broad smiles are positive, however. Be careful to distinguish between genuine broad smiles and "the model's smile." The latter, like the broad smile, exposes both the pearly upper and lowers. But, it lacks the depth, genuineness, and spontaneity of the broad smile, which is often times accompanied by the lifting of the cheeks and crinkling of the eyes. The model's smile is artificial. It is often painted on the faces of celebrities who must maintain a favorable image before the public.

THE EYES HAVE IT: The eyes can also help you read a woman's feelings and attitudes. Direct eye contact, or for that matter, the lack of it can allow you to gauge her interest. Listeners generally engage in more eye contact than those who are speaking. The one doing the talking may divert her eyes to collect a thought. On the other hand, the listener is expected to maintain eye contact. As such, frequent eye evasion generally signifies some form of discomfort. The amount of eye contact—the length and depth of gazing—correlates well with the level of involvement. Increasing eye contact means greater involvement. Interestingly, locking of gazes could signify great interest or, on the other hand, great distaste. Nonetheless, both spell involvement. If you elicit long deep gazes accompanied by pleasant smiles and touching, you may deduce positive interest.

Interestingly, you may have occasion to feel a woman's gaze upon you. It could be at a party, the office, a bus stop, or wherever people are congregated. If you were to meet that gaze, it is her obligation to break eye contact first since, as mentioned previously, it's not polite to stare in our society. However, if eye contact continues, you may be correct in assuming her interest in you, particularly if it is accompanied by a warm smile, which is probably an invitation to an introduction.

HOW TO READ LACK OF INTEREST

Although it's natural that we should all be interested in picking up positive body gestures discussed previously, it would be unwise of us to ignore the less positive body movements. I've seen too many instances where an individual's lack of awareness of unfavorable body gestures led to the wrong course of action, further hindering his chances for establishing a successful relationship. There have been instances when an individual's lack of awareness of unfavorable body gestures resulted in a poor investment of time while attempting to establish a relationship that was never meant to be. So it's important for us to learn the body gestures that communicate absence of favorable interest.

Before we get started, perhaps we should review first what is meant by "lack of interest." As used here, "lack of interest" may be expressed by any one of the following conditions: defensiveness, attempts at self-control, boredom, lack of trust, low level of involvement, suspicion, aggressiveness, skepticism, and so on. After all, a woman who is defensive in your presence really can't be interested in establishing or nurturing a relationship. We must be aware of body gestures that signify any of the above-mentioned conditions so that we can gauge the receptiveness of women to us. In other words, so we can determine whether or not they're interested.

CROSSED ARMS—CLOSED MIND?   Many of the gestures that suggest lack of interest are the opposite of gestures that suggest interest. For example, free use of the arms when communicating can signify openness, confidence, or comfort. The opposite movement—crossed arms—is generally an indication of guardedness, defensiveness, or a closed feeling. You might argue that crossed arms is merely a maneuver to facilitate comfort, and you'll find many devout students of kinesics who will agree with that interpretation. To me, however, crossed arms have always represented an attempt to insulate oneself from the environment or other people, like donning a bulletproof vest to protect oneself from hostility. In order to resolve the issue of comfort versus defensiveness, look for concordant signs when others cross their arms. If a woman's hands are clamped tight against the upper arm or if the hands are balled into fists, you would be safe to conclude defensiveness.

Crossed legs, like crossed arms, usually signifies defensive behavior or at least an attempt at self-control. Again, one may argue that crossing the legs is nothing more than a shift to a more comfortable position. And again, to resolve this issue look for other clues. An accompanying defensive sign is given when a woman with crossed legs leans back deep into a chair, signifying an attempt to solidify her defense to an immovable position or establishing as much physical distance as possible. If crossed legs are coupled with crossed arms, you have further evidence of her desire to cover up. Woe the young man on the make who confronts a woman leaning deep within her chair with crossed legs and arms as she impatiently kicks her foot up and down. It's a good bet she's signaling that she is bored stiff with the environment, the situation, or the company—and wants out!

HEADS UP: A tightly locked jaw coupled with pursed lips, a frown, or even sardonic smile can signify defensiveness or lack of trust. Furrowed brows or one brow raised high above the other could communicate suspicion, deep thought, or even aggression. However, it's doubtful that an initial encounter with someone is going to incite aggressive behavior or hostility unless, perhaps, that individual is under the influence of alcohol or drugs. If that is the case—beware.

The position of the head can provide clues as to how women are receiving you. No doubt you've heard the expression "looking down her nose." That, as you know, is not a favorable gesture. It is represented by the head tilted back, or back and to the side, and is usually accompanied by a locked jaw, pursed lips, or frown and, possibly, furrowed brows. In many instances, crossed arms (and legs, if sitting) may be evidenced. Basically, these gesture clusters suggest she may be skeptical about what you are saying, or that she may distrust you, or that she might simply feel superior.

Rubbing the nose is believed by many to represent rejection or doubt. Now, certainly she may rub her nose because it itches! If there is any doubt about whether she's scratching an itch or subconsciously expressing doubt or rejection, look for reinforcing or contradictory signs. A variant of rubbing the nose is scratching behind, in front, or directly in the ear.

As mentioned earlier, the amount of eye contact she makes with you serves as a pretty good guide to the level of involvement. Absence of eye contact can indicate that she is not attentive. When you are met with a listless listener whose eyes wander everywhere but into your eyes, then you are contending with one uninterested woman.

HOW TO READ FENCE-SITTING

Many times new acquaintances will neither communicate genuine interest nor defensiveness: They're just "fence-sitting." More specifically, they're evaluating what is being received via the ear and eye before making any judgments about whether to continue or terminate an encounter. One note before reviewing these simple body movements: Generally speaking, you can expect to come into contact with this type of behavior in most new encounters. You should not view the fact that you're not being immediately initiated by women into a "friends from the start" relationship as a negative. It's important that the "chemistry" be right for a lasting relationship, as opposed to an acquaintanceship, and it's only through experience, sharing, and evaluation that you might be able to assess the chemistry. Furthermore, the opportunity is always present to take an encounter that begins with mutual evaluation to intimacy, the ultimate relationship.

You'll find the key to most evaluative gestures about the head. Some folks stroke their chin. But, the most notable example is evidenced by Rodin's classic sculpture, "The Thinker." This sculpture exhibits a Greek with his chin poised on his fist, obviously engaged in deep, deep thought. The cheek-in-hand gesture generally signifies contemplation, as does the index finger to the cheek with the remaining fingers employed in cupping the chin in support. She might also remove her glasses when listening, or return them to her nose in an attempt to get a clearer picture of what is being said. A woman may also give away her position by tilting her head and toying with her necklace or an earring.

DON'T JUMP THE GUN

One of the most important principles to adopt when reading body talk is "don't jump the gun." More specifically, don't jump to conclusions based on the interpretation of a single body movement. Just as you wouldn't jump to any conclusions on the weight of a single word, you shouldn't be too quick to conclude anything from a lone gesture. Discipline yourself to read a series of interconnected body movements, or as Gerard I. Nierenberg and Henry H. Calero recommend in their book, *How To Read A Person Like A Book* (Hawthorne Books, Inc., 1971), read "gesture clusters." In short, these so-called gesture clusters are groupings of gestures reflecting attitudes and feelings. To jump to a conclusion based on the interpretation of a single gesture is akin to taking a word, phrase, or sentence out of context. When you do so, you run a significant risk of incorrectly assessing a new contact's feelings.

Here's a brief example that dramatizes the importance of reading a series of body movements as opposed to a single gesture. A friend was at a cocktail party where he was introduced to a group of rather attractive young people. Comfortable in social surroundings, he chimed into the ensuing discussion. As he spoke, he noticed that one of the young women, a statuesque beauty, gazed deeply and fully into his eyes. My friend considers himself to be attractive, interesting, and desirable, and he quickly interpreted her comatose gaze as genuine interest. He deftly separated her from the discussion circle and turned on all the charm he could muster. He was rather taken back when she politely but coolly informed him that she was waiting for her fiance to arrive. She was desperately worried about him because weather conditions had made the roads precarious, and he was taken to speeding in his European sports car.

Unfortunately, my friend mistook a blank stare that really indicated this woman was indifferent to the discussion for unwavering interest. In his ambitious desire to strike up a relationship, he failed to look for supportive gestures and formulated an incorrect assumption on the basis of an impenetrable stare. Had he been alert to other signs, he would have noticed that the gaze was really trance-like, marked by the absence of a single blinking of her eyes. He would have also noticed that her arms were crossed in an attempt to insulate herself from the surroundings. He would have realized that favorable supportive gestures—such as the nodding of the head, smiling, and touching—were not being transmitted.

LISTEN WITH YOUR EYES

This story has a happy ending. Recognizing the predicament this woman was in, he provided needed comfort out of his genuine interest and concern for people. Today, he's a valued friend to this woman—and her fiance. What more can you ask?

Perhaps more importantly, my friend learned a good lesson about "gesture clusters." After considerable reflection, he learned a second important principle as well. Specifically, listening with the eye takes as much effort and concentration as listening with the ear. We filter both aural and visual stimuli based on our interests, and we often tend to get lazy or involved with other things and tune out both. To get the message, the real message, and trace the true progress of your relationships, you have to stay tuned-in, which is not easy. However, take heart! Your ability to stay tuned-in will develop with concentrated effort and practice. Soon you'll find the rewards well worth the effort.

HOW TO SPEAK OUT WITH BODY LANGUAGE

Up till now, we've been studying one facet of body language—reading gestures to assess another's interest in you. But now it's time to introduce another important facet—how to speak out with body language. More specifically, how to use body gestures to win over or turn on today's woman.

Body gestures do affect behavior. Just as someone else's body movements can affect your behavior, your use of body gestures can affect the behavior of others, either favorably or unfavorably. Awareness of the impact body gestures have on women will enable you to monitor your own body movements to bring about a predetermined, desired action.

Hopefully, you won't shy away from this as a Machiavellian ploy designed to manipulate people. There is nothing sinister about it. The fact of the matter is that when you first encounter new acquaintances you don't have a lot of time to create an impression. If they're especially uptight, as we're all apt to be on occasion, the productive use of time for mutual evaluation is significantly reduced. So, if you're to get their undivided attention, you need to learn to be able to put women at ease, for their own sake as well as yours. After all, they're going to benefit from the new relationship, too.

You can tailor your own body gestures to help put today's woman at ease and heighten her receptiveness to you. Recall the body gestures used by the presenter discussed earlier in this chapter. He not only knew how to read body language, he also knew how to speak out with body language. In order to relax his audience and win them over, he carefully orchestrated his body movements. These gestures included unbuttoning his jacket, loosening his tie, smiling, using direct eye contact, and reaching out with open palms. This listing is by no means complete. There are many other ways to put women at ease and win them over.

WATCH YOUR LANGUAGE: Touching is a valuable body movement that can endear oneself to others when used appropriately. Women have a few movements that are unique to their sex. A woman may let her hair down, take off her shoes, and even tuck one leg under her body while sitting to signify she's comfortable in your presence. Chances are if they're comfortable, you will be too. Positive body movements help put others at ease. They communicate that you're open, friendly, and receptive. In creating a favorable environment with positive gestures, coupled with your genuine interest in people, you contribute to putting women at ease and making them more receptive to you.

On the other hand, we all might watch our language so that we don't inadvertently turn others off before we've had a chance to turn them on. Basically, this means avoiding the use of negative, defensive body gestures that can inhibit the development of a positive impression. Our use of body gestures is like a double-edged sword. While positive gestures create a favorable environment, negative gestures can thwart progress. The negative, defensive signs to avoid include crossed arms and/or ankles, clenched hands, listless looking about when others speak, the impatient kicking of the foot while sitting, looking down one's nose, frowning, and so on. We covered these gestures and their meaning previously. Now, try to be aware of your own gestures and determine whether the resultant impact of your movements is the effect you intend to create.

Your body movements can also be used to shore up and spark confidence in yourself while communicating to women that you are self-assured. For example, one evening I had some business to conduct in a rather unfriendly section of the city. By the time my business was completed and I had to return to my car parked several blocks away, night had fallen. I was rather frightened by the dark of night since I had to walk through an area that had witnessed vicious muggings in the recent past. As I began my walk through the dark streets, my body grew gradually erect. Encouraged, I lifted my head high, threw my shoulders back, pulled my muscles taut, and tightened my gut. I strode deliberately to my parking spot. Curiously, these gestures had a rather profound affect upon my personality. I was still concerned about my safety, but my fear had dissolved to caution, and I felt in control of myself.

What happened to me is not unusual. In fact, law enforcement officials advise people to behave similarly when encountering a similar situation with no other options available (like taking a taxi to your car). These actions shore up confidence and self-control. Additionally, they telegraph that you are confident and self-assured to those who may be lurking in the shadows. Of course, social interaction is nowhere near as threatening. If you can spark confidence in such desperate situations by altering your body movements, you may rest assured it can work for you during social encounters. It will provide an added benefit of communicating confidence to the women you meet, creating a favorable impression.

Body movements that can contribute to self-confidence basically are made up of those gestures just mentioned. Pulling yourself together and proceeding in a deliberate fashion can put you in control of yourself, generating confidence and the appearance of self-assurance to others.

HOW TO GREET TODAY'S WOMAN

What should a man do when he meets a woman? It used to be that etiquette demanded that the man let the woman extend her hand first. If she didn't there was to be no shaking hands. However, in these more enlightened days of equality the old etiquette no longer governs. When I meet new women or come in contact with casual acquaintances, I take the initiative in extending my hand. It's my way of saying, "I'm pleased to meet you, and I'm interested in learning more about you."

WOMEN AND THE GRIP: How do women react to a "man-to-man" type handshake? I've asked a number of women, and interestingly, they prefer a man who greets them in a firm (but not bonecrushing) warm and personal manner. Try it and see for yourself. A great deal of importance is given to the handshake, and it's no small wonder. It generally represents the first physical contact with a new acquaintance. As a child I can remember being schooled by my father in the art of the handshake. "Keep it firm, warm and personal," were his words. He was interested in ensuring that I made a good first impression with others.

It got so that I began judging others by the quality of their handshake, based in large part on the importance my father and others placed in the handshake. I wouldn't be surprised if that was the way most people learned to respond to handshakes. Others will often form an opinion of you based on your handshake. Whether their opinion is right or wrong, it's important for you to be aware of what their expectations are so you won't convey an incorrect impression.

There are a few different types of handshake. I'd rather not belabor this. The important point is that women will judge you according to the way you shake hands during a greeting. Here are brief descriptions of each of the handshake types:

The Pumper: He grabs your hand and pumps vigorously, as though he's attempting to draw water from deep within a well. One's general impression is to label this joker a "klutz."

The Iron Clamp: Out goes your hand, and in the time it takes to blink an eye he clamps down like a vise. The sadist generally won't let go until either your eyes begin to pop or he hears a few bones crack. Color this pseudo macho-man "insensitive."

The Controller: He uses both hands. Either he'll grab your hand in both of his or he'll bring his left hand up to your right arm. Then he shakes and he shakes and he shakes. So you shake back, and then you loosen your grip. But he still shakes and shakes and shakes until he's ready to let you go. While he may believe he's conveying a warm personality, he's most often perceived as being suffocating and artificial.

The Dead Fish: This is the bottom of the barrel. Nothing can help you should others view you as a dead fish handshaker. The hand that lies limp and lifeless. What's worse, it's generally perceived as cold and clammy. Others view this type of handshaker as weak, cold, impersonal, and not really interested in people.

Making a good first impression is really not difficult. Just keep the handshake firm, warm and personal. Look into her eyes, smile, use her name, and show genuine interest.

HOW TO BECOME FLUENT IN BODY LANGUAGE

Unfortunately, there's no easy way or shortcut to learn body language. You must speak the language if you're going to learn and play it for all it's worth. This is not a difficult language to learn. However, this book, or a hundred others, won't give you the skills you need. Reading will make you aware of the many facets of body language, but you have to put that awareness to work. Books cannot develop the skills, they're acquired on the playing field of life and social interaction. One can read scores of books on a wide range of subjects, from playing golf to flying an airplane. But, the point is that you must put into practice what you read if you're ever going to be proficient in swinging a nine iron or landing an aircraft. To become fluent in body language you have to use the language and put into practice what you're learning.

Two years ago I attended a management seminar designed to increase awareness of interpersonal skills. In order to heighten our awareness of body language, the seminar director showed clips from an old movie, without the sound. Our exercise was to determine via the body gestures what was going on. This is an excellent exercise. All you need to do is turn the sound off your TV and *voilà!* Tune in some of the old-time movies or the popular soap operas. Both the old-time movies and the soaps use more than their fair share of body movements to supplement and compliment the dialogue. They run the gamut of emotions. So, turn off the sound on your TV from time to time and try to determine what's happening.

Another suggestion is to set time aside each day to study the body language of friends, relatives, and associates. We tend to place greater importance on words. After all, we're a nation founded on words. So, at first it's going to take concerted effort to focus on body movements. Before engaging in social interaction, whether at home, play, or work, remind yourself to pick up another's body gestures. Examine whether the body gestures are in harmony with the spoken word and what the body says when the mouth says nothing.

In order to improve your use of body gestures in putting others at ease and opening them up to your personality, all you need is a mirror and a little practice. Just stand before a mirror and carry on a conversation with yourself. As you do so, practice using positive body movements until they come naturally.

Before long, you can be fluent in body language, and that fluency will enable you to identify women who are open to new relationships, gain feedback as to whether you're being accepted by them, spark added confidence, and open up today's woman to you.

CHAPTER NINE

HOW TO BUILD A WINNING IMAGE WITH WOMEN

Your image is important. In fact, one's personal image is so important that image consultants have sprung up to provide advice on how to go about developing a "winning" image. The demand has been so great for this service that the number of image consultants is increasing. Editorial Services Co. of N.Y., publisher of the directory of personal image consultants, listed just thirty-seven specialists in 1977. Only one year later the listing increased to 100. Today there are well over that number of specialists who give advice on everything from wardrobe selection to personal public relations.

The importance of a person's image in achieving success is becoming more widely recognized in all facets of life. Consider politics as an example. Many historians credit John F. Kennedy's win over Richard M. Nixon in the 1960 presidential election to the more youthful and favorable image conveyed by the late President Kennedy during their highly publicized debates on television. In addition, an article appearing in the Feb. 23, 1979 edition of *The Wall Street Journal* reported that former President Carter's aides were looking to bolster the President's image as a strong leader. This came on the heels of criticism from the American public regarding Mr. Carter's decisions dealing with foreign and domestic problems. However, the Carter aides failed to improve the former President's image as a strong leader. The rest is history. Mr. Carter was defeated in his bid for reelection to the presidency by Ronald Reagan.

The entertainment industry offers yet another highly visible example of the importance of image in achieving success. Many of today's movie stars have cultivated an image that appeals to a specific segment of the viewing population. The late John Wayne is a case in point. He built an image that epitomized America's rugged individualism, a man of action, integrity, "true grit," and idealism by the parts he chose to play. He built a cinema image that spilled into his personal life of the good guy who comes out of nowhere to conquer evil and right any wrongs, regardless of the risk to himself. That image was sufficiently credible and appealing to successfully attract millions of moviegoers and fuel an illustrious career that spanned generations.

Your personal image is important. It has an impact on your eventual success with women. It has an impact on the type and number of intimate new partners you'll attract. It affects the way today's woman will respond to you.

Everyone projects an image. The way women respond to you mirrors the image you consciously or subconsciously project. Your image is shaped by your posture, physical appearance and condition, business and social behavior, dress, grooming habits, the company you keep, your apparent energy level, and even your name. Each of these factors will influence the type and number of women you'll be able to attract.

Although everyone projects an image, it's important that you convey a positive image. It's important that you get women to view you favorably if you are going to make headway in developing intimate new relationships with the type of women you desire. So, you need to create an image that is capable of eliciting a positive reaction.

YOUR IMAGE STARTS WITH YOU

If you are going to improve your chances for success, you need to plan carefully to develop a winning image. You can't depend on luck to help you find new partners. You need to cultivate an image that's unique to you, and nothing is more unique or right for you than an image that starts out with who you really are. Basically, what we're talking about is steering your image in the right direction so you can attract more of the type of women you desire. This does not consist of creating a fictitious personality. That would be outright misrepresentation, and misrepresentation is eventually uncovered, resulting in unnecessary embarrassment, hurt feelings, and hostility.

The advertising business spends thousands of hours developing, producing, and airing one 30-second commercial. The time is spent on determining what kind of impression (image) to make on the target audience, and ensuring that the message conveys the intended impression (image). Likewise, we need to take the time to think through the image we want to project (purposeful, confident, successful, and so on) and work to ensure we convey our intended message.

Here are a few suggestions to help you project a winning image:

WHAT'S IN A NAME?

You'd be surprised, but there's a lot more to a name than one would imagine. A name signifies a basic set of attributes, characteristics, and personality types to others. This isn't to suggest that you need to go out and change your name, but you might be more sensitive to the nickname you adopt or allow your friends to call you. For example, if your name is Vincent you may prefer the nickname Jim to Vinny. Or, you might prefer Jim to Jamie if your name is James. Perhaps you may just prefer being called James. Each of these names has a profound impact upon how women view you. Many will view Jamie as a boy (perhaps even a momma's boy), but James is adult. It's strong. It's elegant.

Also, drop any adolescent nicknames. I have a neighbor who must be forty-eight years of age, and yet his family and old friends insist on calling this man, who is married and has three children,

"Junior." Now that's not very suave. For that matter neither is Butch (a ruffian), Mac (a non-entity) or Skip (a bright-eyed, bushy-tailed kid). What type of impression do you think women will get from these names? What kind of women do you believe they'll attract?

Your name will not only affect how others view you but indirectly upon your own behavior. It's no coincidence that the "Juniors" I've met don't come off as being very mature, independent, or dynamic. They generally behave like kids, deferring to others for direction and leadership.

PHYSICAL CONDITIONING

Your physical condition can also influence the image you project. I know that when I exercise I feel good about myself and better about everything else as well. I'm optimistic about life, and everyone and everything that touches it. It gives me increased energy that's clearly visible to others. Moreover, fitness exudes a healthy, dynamic image. Others associate a lean, hard look with a lean, hard mind.

Consider for a moment the image that obesity creates. Generally, most people will respond with "Lazy, slovenly, gluttonous, soft, self-indulgent, undisciplined." Now, this isn't to say that if you're overweight you have no chance to establish new relationships. Quite the contrary. The principles discussed throughout this book will help you make contact and develop relationships with women. What this does mean, however, is that you're carrying excess baggage whenever you attempt to make productive contact with women you desire. You're strapping yourself with the needless burden of the unfavorable image that an overweight condition projects.

So, if you are on the plump side, shed those excess pounds. Start by cutting down your caloric intake. There are plenty of proven diets around and if you have difficulty finding or choosing one, ask your doctor. Also, get involved in an exercise program or activity that will help you burn off excess calories and improve your muscle tone. Get involved in activities that fit into your likes and habits or you'll soon tire of them and drop out of your program. The activities that seem to work best for most people are group activities that encourage involvement and motivate you to stick with the program. As an added benefit, they provide you with an additional opportunity to meet women who are enrolled in the same program.

DRESS

First impressions count, and one of the first impressions women get is based upon how we're dressed. Men who appear successful, confident, and stylish generally make more favorable impressions on today's women, improving their opportunities to develop new relationships. Dress can have an impact upon the way women view you and even how you feel about yourself. Let's not be hypocritical. We often judge women on the basis of their dress. Certain blouses, hairstyles, and jewelry project femininity, and others suggest seductiveness. Consequently, our behavior towards these women is affected by the image their dress projects. Likewise, your wardrobe can have a profound impact on your ability to attract women.

This isn't to suggest that you sell your stereo or mortgage your car to raise $5,000 so you can purchase a new wardrobe. Try to make the best with what you have. However, if you need to spend a few dollars to update your wardrobe, it'll be well worth the investment. Companies invest in advertising to build their images and sell their products. Look at your wardrobe not as a self-indulgent or needless luxury, but as a worthwhile investment in building a winning image with women. Your dress can help you look successful, and sexy, and can even compensate for physical characteristics (such as being short or heavy) you'd like to overcome. Improving your dress isn't going to make you a real ladies' man but it can increase your opportunities for meeting women by making you appear more attractive. Also, it will work to keep women from tuning you out before you have a fighting chance to turn them on.

If you have difficulty selecting a wardrobe that appropriately projects a winning image, ask for help. You can get help from friends, sales personnel, even your sister. In fact, John T. Molloy, the self-proclaimed first dress engineer and author of *Dress for Success* (Warner Books, Inc., 1975), advises that if you want to attract women you should simply let them pick out your clothing. They'll select clothing that will make you appear more sexually appealing. He relates a story about Don Juan, the world's foremost lover, to support his advice:

> "When Don Juan was on his death bed he was giving advice to a young man who wished to follow in his rather-to-be-envied footsteps. When it came to the discussion of clothing the young man should wear to attract women, Don Juan told him simply to attract one woman and let her pick out his clothing. Thus clothed, the young man could then pick out all the women he desired."

HOW TO DRESS SUCCESSFULLY: Here are some pointers that will help you clothe yourself to appeal to and attract today's woman:

1. *Shop at reputable clothing stores.* Generally, they sell quality merchandise that isn't going to look shabby after a few cleanings or, worse yet, after you've been wearing the clothes for a few hours. They stock the latest fashions and colors as well. Their sales help are usually paid on a commission basis, meaning that they tend to know what they're talking about and want you to be satisfied with your purchases so they might sell you additional merchandise later. You can count on them to help you select colors and merchandise that mask undesirable and accentuate positive physical characteristics. Finally, the more reputable clothing stores can afford to employ skilled tailors to ensure your clothes are perfectly fitted.

2. *Get your clothes properly fitted.* Don't overlook the fit of your clothes. It's essential for your clothes to fit properly or you'll fail to convey an attractive appearance. There's nothing more tacky than ill-fitting clothes, whether they be too loose or tight, long or short. The way your clothes fit can be as important as the clothes you wear. Be sure to have a tailor fit your clothes, not a salesperson. Also, don't make full payment for your clothes until you are satisfied the alterations were properly made.

• If you are purchasing pants make sure they break slightly over your shoes. In fact, it would be helpful if you wore the shoes you plan on wearing with the pants for the fitting. Also, check the waist and seat for a well-tailored, yet comfortable, fit. Use your judgment when being fitted. If it's not comfortable then it isn't fitted properly, so don't buy it.

• If it is a sports jacket you are after, check to make sure the collar fits against the neck, and does not hang away from it. Check to make sure the lapels are in fashion. Often times bargains can be illusory if you're not aware of current fashions. It's not much of a bargain if you purchase a jacket whose lapel is out of style. If you're of thin or average build, have the waist of the jacket taken in slightly to accentuate your chest and shoulders. If, on the other hand, you're a heavy figure give yourself some room at the waist. With regard to the sleeves, they should come down to the wrist bone. The sides of the jacket should fall to a point where the fingers of your hands curl with your arms hanging down.

• When buying shirts, make sure the tails are sufficiently long so that they don't pull out of your pants. A shirt hanging out of your pants will give you a disheveled and sloppy appearance.

• Don't be afraid to use your tailor. Get his advice. Consult with him about ways your clothes can be fitted to bring out your positive attributes and downplay any undesirable physical characteristics.

3. *When you shop, wear the accessories you would to compliment your purchase.* This helps three ways. First, the resulting outfit has a coordinated look with matching fabrics and patterns. Second, by wearing your accessories (especially shoes) you get a better fitting.

Third, you generally look better when you go shopping and receive better service from sales personnel. In other words, you project an image of being fashionable, successful, and of sufficient financial means to warrant extra sales attention and consideration. You'll find that sales people will be willing to invest more time with you in anticipation of building their clientele with another loyal customer.

4. *Don't be sold.* It's one thing to buy what you need but another to recklessly spend your hard-earned and scarce funds on items you just don't need. The best way to prevent "being sold" is to carefully plan your wardrobe. Take inventory of what you have and what articles of clothing you need. When you do go shopping you will be buying for your needs, not on a whim or under pressure of a pushy and persuasive sales person. This will help you stretch your dollars further and help you quickly establish a wardrobe of coordinated outfits.

GOOD GROOMING PRACTICES

Your grooming habits tell women quite a bit about you. If you look disheveled and sloppy, chances are you are going to be perceived as being disheveled and sloppy. Yet, you can vastly improve your appearance and appeal with a few good grooming techniques.

START AT THE TOP: Let's start at the top—with your hair. One of my closest friends has a set of ears that stick out like barn doors. They give him an appearance of being a yokel. It's a shame because he is basically a handsome fellow, and smart and considerate of others. But those big, floppy ears make him look as though he doesn't have much gray matter between them. He went to a hairstylist who showed him how to mask this undesirable characteristic by allowing his hair to grow out over his ears. He took the hairstylist's advice and today he looks like a different person. His hair overcomes the floppy ears. It helps create an image of being easygoing and down-home, whereas before he looked rather daffy. This points out the importance of your hairstyle. If you can afford it, get your hair styled! The stylist can help you decide which length and style best suits your face so you can accentuate your positive features and compensate for any characteristics women will not find appealing. Also, having your hair styled will help it keep easier. A shampoo and blow dry will keep you neat and together throughout the day.

CLEAN TEETH, CLEAN FACE: A smile is like magic. It can light up your face and make you look your best. Also, it helps convey an image of friendliness and basic human warmth. And your smile looks best when your teeth are cleaned. If your teeth aren't cleaned by your dentist or hygienist every six or twelve months they tend to lose their luster and take on a dull, yellow appearance (particularly if you are a heavy coffee drinker or smoker). This could understandably project an unfavorable image to the women you hope to attract. Many of the popular toothpastes help to brighten your teeth, but nothing beats a professional cleaning. So get to your dentist every six to twelve months and brighten up your smile.

Skin blemishes, acne and blackheads can adversely affect your image. In fact, they have their most notable impact on your psychological well-being. They generally leave people feeling self-conscious and uncomfortable in a contact situation, and undermine their confidence and chance for success. Advertised skin care products can help minimize blemishes, but if you have a difficult case don't hesitate to consult a dermatologist.

Mustaches and beards are readily accepted and appreciated by today's women. Many women are "turned on" by a manly display of facial hair. The key is to keep your mustache or beard neatly trimmed and groomed. It not only serves to give you a cleaner, neater appearance, but also highlights your mustache and beard.

You'd be surprised at the number of women who notice a man's hands. Your hands can convey sensitivity and/or a sense of strength. They can tell people whether you work in an office or outdoors. Given the interest of women in a man's hands, it makes good sense to keep your nails cleaned and trimmed. If your hobby is working under the hood of your car make sure you use products designed to clean away the grease and oil from under the fingernails and from your hands.

YOUR POSTURE

Your posture tells people a lot about you. I recall reading an article about victims of muggers. Muggers claimed they made victims of people who appeared to be ambling about without a sense of purpose. They went after people with heads hung low, hands in pockets and shoulders stooped. They avoided anyone who strode briskly and purposefully, people who walked with shoulders thrown back and swaggered with confidence. The reason for the muggers' behavior was the image projected by the potential victim. Quite simply, the muggers claimed that those who ambled aimlessly would most likely be passive and, as such, be easy marks. But those who carried themselves confidently, conveying an image of energy, led the muggers to believe these people might take action in response to a threat. Don't overlook your posture, it makes a definitive statement about your personality.

To give an impression of energy, success, and a sense of purpose, keep your head up and focus your eyes straight ahead. Stride purposefully and briskly and keep your hands out of your pockets. You'll look alive with energy and strength. On the other hand, avoid slouching your shoulders. It will make you look sloppy, slow moving, and lacking in energy.

When you take a chair, sit. Don't plop down or slump in a chair. Your purpose should be to create an image of alertness, aliveness, a sense of energy. Let your body speak well of you, and women will respond with interest and enthusiasm.

ADDITIONAL IMAGE ENHANCERS

A caring image is important and can open many a door to a woman's heart. One way to show you care is to remember everything you can about the women with whom you make contact. Remember their interests, likes and dislikes, what they were wearing, who may have introduced you, how you met, and so on. You don't need to take a memory course if you don't have a photographic memory. Jot down points of interest following your encounters and review your notes before you get together again. When you remember, you show a woman you believe she's important and that you care about her attitudes, feelings, desires, and person.

Another way to enhance your image is to create an impression of energy. Women flock to men of energy and enthusiasm. Your unbounded energy will flow over and affect others in a positive manner. Energy suggests you are active, competent, and an achiever. If you're not one of those people whose energy seems to overflow naturally, rest up before you go out on the town in search of new contacts. Also, try to segment your day based on the tasks or projects before you. This will serve to motivate and encourage you with successes to accomplish each task before you. Also, it will help focus your efforts and, as such, heighten your energy. Other helpful hints include: Change your work pace and mix activities throughout the day (if possible).

Yes, your image is important, but don't try to be all things to all women. It's important that your image flow from who you actually are and not be a fabrication based on what you believe women would like you to be. This reminds me of a famous singer of the early '70's. His songs and life style conveyed an image of sensitivity to feelings, caring for others and our society, and a wholesome, down-to-earth attitude. Unfortunately, his record sales began to wane in favor of acid and punk rock and the wave of disco. To bolster his sales, he undertook a campaign to change his image. He talked about using drugs and his estrangement from his lovely wife. He even changed the type of music he played and sang. But, he failed to convince the new, broader audience he sought. Worse yet, because he tried to be all things to all people, his image suffered among his previous fans and he found himself with less rather than more appeal.

Your image can have a profound impact on attracting women. Everything about you makes a statement about who and what you are. With a little care to the factors discussed throughout this chapter, like dress and grooming habits, you can do much to create a winning image with today's woman.

CHAPTER TEN

HOW TO DEVELOP LASTING RELATIONSHIPS

A perfect match—that's what everyone said about Frank and Ellen. Frank was dark, handsome, well-built, articulate, and the hero of the campus gridiron. He was the "all-American boy," voted "Most Likely to Succeed" by his classmates, and destined (in the eyes of everyone) to one day make a major contribution to society. And Ellen was the envy of everyone who knew her. She was an honor student, assistant editor of the school newspaper, and campus beauty queen. It seemed inevitable that these two beautiful and talented people would be attracted to each other and marry. Or was it? Even before they could celebrate their first wedding anniversary Frank and Ellen filed for divorce.

The telephone wires rang with cries of "What went wrong?" We were all shocked. After all, how could their marriage possibly fail? They appeared to have everything two people could ever hope to have going for them.

What happened to Frank and Ellen isn't all that uncommon. Today there is one divorce in every two marriages. "Down with marriage," cry those whose trip to the altar failed to give birth to the joyful relationship they expected. It isn't the institution of marriage that's failing us—it's our system of establishing relationships.

ILL-FITTING RELATIONSHIPS

Relationships are essential to living, not just to fulfill sexual needs but for our psychological and emotional well-being. We all desperately need intimacy and love in today's cool, impersonal corporate climate where we are often reduced to numbers and consumers, rather than people with important emotional needs. We need someone to love if nothing more than to confirm our identity and sense of worth.

Unfortunately, our hunger for love makes us behave in ways we believe will avoid rejection in a relationship. It would be easy to criticize a woman for her "courting behavior" after the relationship sours. However, the truth of the matter is we're all guilty, to some degree, of contributing to deception and false illusions when courting. Here are some of the pitfalls you should avoid as they contribute to involving us in ill-fitting relationships.

IGNORING DIFFERENCES: Our fear of losing love will often cause us to overlook differences and latch on to unimportant similarities. Sid and Shelley are prime examples. Sid is Jewish, while Shelley is a devout Irish Catholic. Although Sid does not object to marriage, he would prefer to wait because he is studying to be a doctor and needs to devote all his energies toward this pursuit. Moreover, if he were to marry in the near future, he certainly would not want children right away. He couldn't afford to have his wife out of work given the incredible costs of medical school. He is also interested in several childless years following marriage while he builds up his practice. On the other hand, Shelley is ready to get married and leave her job in the corporate steno pool to care for a husband and brood of children. She herself is one of several children and would enjoy a large family.

Sid and Shelley meet at a popular New York night spot. They are attracted to each other almost immediately. Sid is taken in by her fair Irish beauty, petite figure, and lusty exuberance. Shelley in turn is attracted to Sid's dark good looks, soft-spoken manner, and seeming sensitivity. They dance through the night comparing and discussing similarities in the hope of establishing a more lasting relationship. They both like to dance, they agree. Travel is a shared ambition, they nod. All the while they sidestep the fact that Sid enjoys investigating the historical significance of a locale, whereas Shelley is interested in the purely recreational aspect of the beaches, restaurants, and nightspots. They both grew up in Queens and enjoy strong family ties. They both enjoy wine.

Sid and Shelley are soon caught up in each other emotionally and physically, and begin dating regularly. They dig deeply into the relationship to establish similarities. Meanwhile, they sweep under the rug the truly meaningful differences: their religions, family and cultural backgrounds, educational experiences, aspirations for the future, and interests. Sid and Shelley marry, and Shelley has the marriage annulled shortly thereafter. Both are bitter and disillusioned with the relationship. Yet, it isn't the marriage that failed. The relationship was a poor fit from the start. Sid and Shelley never really had a chance, but they allowed themselves to become involved by ignoring meaningful differences and fueling the relationship with unimportant similarities.

PLAYACTING: We engage in playacting to preserve a relationship. There are basically two ways this can be done. The first is to put our best face forward, all smiles and sweetness so that others get a favorable impression of us. What this amounts to is being on your best behavior at all times. It consists of submerging your true feelings, emotions and lifestyle so as to avoid conflict or creating an unfavorable impression. Your intentions may be honorable, but this amounts to "misleading advertising."

A second form of playacting is when one behaves as he believes his partner would like him to behave. Phil and Michelle are an interesting example. Phil loves the outdoors—skiing, camping, backpacking, mountaineering, just about anything that gets him out under the sky. Michelle is a real homebody. She prefers to watch

TV, curl up with a book or her needlepoint, or just listen to music. Phil and Michelle met at a party and were attracted to one another. During their courtship Phil acquainted Michelle with the great outdoors. He took her canoeing, hiking through the woods, cross-country skiing, and camping in the wilds. While Michelle detested sleeping under the stars and being exposed to the elements, she playacted, behaving the way she believed Phil wanted her to behave. She behaved in a way that she knew would please Phil. Unfortunately, their relationship came under storm shortly after they were married. As a wedding gift Phil bought a few hundred dollars worth of ski equipment for Michelle. And was he surprised when Michelle bridled at a ski vacation he planned for the both of them.

Jim is another example of someone who trapped himself in an ill-fitting relationship with Susan. In this case it was Jim who was the homebody. Usually worn out from a hard day working on the loading dock for a railroad company, Jim would come home exhausted. His idea of recreation was downing a few beers as he sat mesmerized before his TV and the broadcasted sporting event of the day. On the other hand, Susan enjoyed getting out to nightclubs, dancing and partying into the wee hours of the morning. In courting Susan, Jim managed to muster additional energy and tear himself away from the TV sports scene to go cavorting with Susan. You can well imagine what came after their wedding. Susan couldn't pry Jim away from his TV. The result: More fodder for the divorce courts.

STEREOTYPING: You meet a woman who looks like the actress Suzanne Sommers. It just so happens you're a great fan of Ms. Sommers. You're wild about her screen personality, which you judge is sexy, amusingly daffy, and friendly. So, based on this woman's appearance and your favorable impression of Suzanne Sommers you initiate a relationship. But, does her physical appearance mean your friend will have a similar image and personality as the screen star? Certainly not. If you deceive yourself by stereotyping, you could be held responsible for contributing to nurturing an ill-fitting relationship.

While all of us need love and desire to share intimacy with others, ignoring differences, playacting, and stereotyping are likely to lead to trouble. While they may serve to camouflage an ill-fitting relationship, they are very likely to backfire, releasing frustration, and even hostility.

HOW TO FIND
THE RIGHT SOMEONE(S)

The key to nurturing a lasting relationship is clear: You must find the right someone(s) for you. Not someone who meets some romantic notion others may have established for beauty or behavior based on what's pushed upon us from the media. Instead, someone who meets your unique, total human needs, not just your sexual needs—your needs for friendship, support, understanding and affection.

I suggest the plural "someones" because there are many women who could satisfy your needs. There is no one relationship tailor-made in heaven to the exclusion of all others. We're all capable of nurturing relationships with a variety of women (not all at the same time, of course). The relationship you may someday have is just one of the many you can enjoy when you find the right "someones" for you.

Before you go looking for the right someone(s), you need to be clear on your objectives. You need to know who you are, what you like, and what you need. Moreover, you must be clear about your needs versus the nice-to-have wants. Is it a need or a want that the woman you marry be a good cook? Homemaker? Lover? Additionally, you need to establish selection criteria compatible with your own personality and lifestyle. If you prefer to sit home and watch TV, then perhaps you shouldn't make any arbitrary demands that your woman be academically and intellectually oriented. You may find, in that case, you have nothing in common.

And in order to know what you really need you have to know yourself. The importance of knowing thyself—what you really want versus what you think you want—is brought home by Mel Krantzler, author of *Creative Divorce* (Signet, 1974).* In analyzing rejections he suffered with women following his divorce, Krantzler had to come to terms with the type of relationship he really wanted and what he was doing to attract the kind of women he desired. Here's what he has to say:

> "I was forced to acknowledge that what I *said* I wanted in a relationship and what I *really* wanted were two different things.
>
> *I said I wanted a woman who was interesting as a person, yet I still viewed women as sex objects and second-class citizens. They were there primarily to listen to my problems and to take to bed.
>
> *I said I wanted a woman to view me with no illusory expectations, but what I really wanted was a woman who would buy my own illusions about myself.
>
> *I said I wanted an open relationship of shared feelings, but I continued to assume I knew what a woman was thinking or feeling without bothering to ask her. She had to live up to my own set of fantasies; never mind what she was really like.
>
> *I said I was ready for a mature relationship between two adults, but what I really wanted was someone to take care of me. I was confusing a home-cooked meal with love."

HOW TO ESTABLISH
SUCCESSFUL RELATIONSHIPS

Knowing yourself and what you really need in a relationship will help you find the right someone(s) and build a lasting relationship. But Krantzler's comments also bring out the importance you play in

* Mel Krantzler is also the author of *Learning to Love Again* (New York: T.Y. Crowell, 1978); and *Creative Marriage* (New York: McGraw-Hill, 1980).

establishing a successful relationship. He freely admits he behaved like a "chauvinist pig" in his relationships with women. He failed to acknowledge the needs, wants and desires of his partners. In short, he failed to be "other directed," focusing selfishly on himself at the expense of the women with whom he hoped to establish a relationship. If a relationship is going to develop into long-lasting intimacy, both parties must give and receive value. Both parties must have their needs satisfied, or the relationship will fail. You play an equal part in the success of a relationship. You have an obligation to treat your partner with love, respect, caring, considerateness, and interest. *You must treat your partner as you would like to be treated.*

MARRIAGE AS A MODEL

What makes a successful marriage can give us valuable insight into what can make a successful relationship. In her article, *Do You Have What it Takes to Make a Good Marriage?* in the October, 1980 *Ladies Home Journal,* Sally W. Olds talks about the personality profiles of successful marriage partners. These profiles are based on work by two social scientists who studied families to identify ingredients and personality traits that make a marriage (relationship) work. Here's what they learned:

ENJOY DOING FOR OTHERS: People in good relationships are giving people who enjoy doing things for each other. This is what I like to refer to as an outgrowth of love: You get pleasure out of doing things to make your partner happy. For example, the fellow who vacuums around the apartment or makes his partner breakfast in bed satisfies his own needs while he satisfies the needs of his loved one. In making her happy he is making himself happy. He gets pleasure in giving.

COMMITMENT TO SUCCESS: They have a real commitment to making the relationship work. In other words, those couples who enjoy lasting, truly intimate relationships work hard at making those relationships successful. Unfortunately, many people make the mistake of believing they can stop wooing their partner after the courtship is over. Let's face it, if the relationship is going to work you must be committed to making it work. It's sad that many couples will spruce themselves up and put their best face forward while they're courting and simply neglect their appearance and partners after the wedding. Then, after the divorce they're predictably back to sprucing themselves up and putting their best face forward again as they prepare to snare yet another victim. If they only put the same energy into the marriage as they did in the courtship they may have been able to build a lasting relationship.

EQUALITY—AVOID SUFFOCATION: They see themselves as equals and work to preserve their unique identities. Successful couples do not allow the relationship to suffocate their identities. They recognize their partner's need for independence to pursue his or her interests and cultivate his or her values. They give each other ample space and time. In doing so they avoid two cardinal sins that serve to undermine a relationship. They are not possessive nor do they try to make their partner over like themselves.

Possessiveness is suffocating. It acts as a roadblock to personal growth. It prevents a partner from being herself and pursuing her interests. Take Elliott and Dianne as an example. Dianne has always enjoyed playing tennis with her girlfriends. She is a tournament-class player. When she met Elliott, however, he demanded that she spend every available moment with him, including the time each week she usually played tennis. I happened to see Dianne recently, and she looked unhappy. She complained bitterly about her loss of personal freedom. While she loves Elliott, I know the relationship just isn't going to last much longer.

Attempting to make your partner over to your specifications isn't going to work either. First, we just can't change from what we are to someone else's preconceived notion of what she'd like us to be. Second, if we can't accept a person for who she is then you might as well forget the relationship. Attempting to make another over will make her miserable, generating unnecessary frustrations and open hostility. Moreover, attempting to make another over is really an insult. It suggests you believe she is not worthy or up to your standards and, as such, damages her sense of worth and value.

COMMUNICATION: They communicate. For a relationship to be successful you need to be able to communicate with each other. You need to be able to share feelings, opinions, and thoughts. One of the major problems that emerges when couples whose relationship is on the skids seek counseling is that they have not openly communicated their feelings. Instead they have let problems and concerns build up until they explode in a rage of name-calling and inflammatory, bitter, biting remarks. As you can well imagine, these outbursts create hurt feelings and undermine each other's confidence in his or her ability to love and be loved. They also serve to chip away at the mutual trust that serves as the bedrock of all good relationships.

COMMUNICATE FOR A LASTING RELATIONSHIP

The importance of maintaining open communications cannot be overstated. It's essential to building a lasting, intimate relationship. In fact, women reveal in the June, 1980 issue of the *Ladies Home Journal* study, "*Marriage Today*" that the ability to communicate is important in a relationship. Not only is your ability to communicate important but what you say and how you say it will also affect your relationship. It's certainly a good idea to communicate your affection and love for your partner. You should try to communicate positive feelings frequently and spontaneously. They'll be greatly appreciated and the feelings genuinely returned. Don't wait for a holiday occasion to express your feelings, do it when the moment or thought strikes you.

CLEAR THE AIR

Likewise, you need to be open about problems in the relationship. We just can't sweep problems under the rug and hope they will be forgotten or work themselves out without any help from us. They may lie dormant for a short time, but they tend to build up, causing hostility and resentment. That's why it is important to face up to any problems or conflicts and resolve them as they crop up. But how we air our feelings is as important as the problem itself. Here are some suggestions that can help you clear the air tactfully and improve your relationship:

BE POSITIVE: Don't criticize the person but instead talk about the behavior you find troubling and sprinkle your comments with plenty of positives. Personal criticism is destructive. It puts others on the defensive and causes a great deal of resentment. Dale Carnegie, author of the famous book, *How to Win Friends and Influence People* (New York: Pocket Books, 1936) warns:

> "Let's realize that criticisms are like homing pigeons. They always return home. Let's realize that the person we are going to correct and condemn will probably justify himself, and condemn us in return ... When dealing with people let us remember we are not dealing with creatures of logic. We are dealing with creatures of emotion, creatures bristling with prejudices, and motivated by pride and vanity. And criticism is a dangerous spark—a spark that is liable to cause an explosion in the powder magazine of pride."

One way to avoid personal criticism is to talk about your feelings, not the other person's shortcomings. When you refer to another's weaknesses you criticize and set up a potentially explosive situation. Also, make sure you reinforce another's positive attributes before you identify the behavior you find troublesome. This will calm the waters and establish that you believe she is worthwhile. As well, it will get your partner to listen as opposed to tuning you out.

Here's an example of a problem and how we might handle the situation. It's a total fabrication, but it can provide insights into handling legitimate gripes. Your girlfriend has the unfortunate habit of telling you how to behave and what you should do, even in public. You know she means well, but she makes you feel like a fool. One night you're dining with a few couples at a cozy neighborhood restaurant when you commit a social blunder at the table. Overcome by your appetite you relish a bowl of minestrone soup with slurps of delight. As opposed to kicking you gently under the table your woman friend says, "Frankie, don't be such a slob. You know better than to slurp at your food like a famished animal." Despite mixed feelings of profound embarrassment and rage, you make a joke of the situation and the other members of your party go on to talk about another subject.

Sensitive to her feelings, you wait until you are both alone to air your gripe so as not to cause your friend the undue embarrassment you suffered. It goes like this:

YOU	EXPLANATION OF BEHAVIOR
"Joanne, I'm really crazy about you. I enjoy having you close to me when we're out with friends. You're so much fun and an interesting conversationalist."	You start by reassuring your friend that you value her as a person by citing some positive behavior or attributes. This gets her to listen to what you have to say and defuses what could be an explosive situation by reaffirming her worth to you. In order to be successful your positive comments must be *sincere*.
"But I get so angry whenever you correct me in front of friends or out in public. It makes me feel so inadequate, like an incompetent fool, and causes me a great deal of embarrassment."	Note: You tell her what behavior bothers you as opposed to being critical of her. This keeps her from feeling criticized or attacked and helps her focus on the problem as opposed to building a counter argument to defend herself. Moreover, you tell her how her behavior makes you feel. This helps her see things from your viewpoint, improving her sensitivity to your feelings.
"I know you do it because you care for me. You want me to be at my	You give her additional reassurance that you value and do not think

best and I appreciate that because I want to be at my best too."

"But I prefer you wait and tell me of things that bother you when we're alone together. When we're out of earshot of others ... and when you can reassure me that you love me too (said with a smile)."

poorly of her for this behavior. This too keeps her from feeling criticized and attacked.

You give her a solution to the problem. You let her know how she can please you in a calm, quiet manner. There are no threats or demands that can provoke an all-out verbal battle that will leave you both embittered and without solving the problem.

In summary, when you have occasion to air a gripe:

- *Be calm.* It will help you think straight and keep others from getting riled.
- *Don't criticize the person.* Rather, talk about the behavior that bothers you. This will keep others from feeling attacked and rejected. It also helps get them to listen and focus on the objectionable behavior.
- *Sprinkle your comments with sincere and genuine positives.* This reassures others that you value and respect them. It also keeps them from feeling threatened.
- *Don't make threats.* Threats provoke anger and cause people to react in a hostile manner, if nothing else but to save face.
- *Tell others how the objectionable behavior makes you feel.* It helps others see things from your viewpoint, improving their sensitivity to your feelings.
- *Be nice.* Be considerate of her feelings. After all, you're not interested in hurting her. And you certainly don't want to alienate her.

And if you're pulled into an argument, listen—really listen—to what others have to say. You also need to understand what needs she has. Many times a compromise position can be worked out.

Above all, keep away from irrational and destructive ploys, like name-calling and trying to shout her down. This solves nothing and can leave you both feeling hurt, embittered, and hostile. The old idea "count to ten before you speak" is a good one to adopt. It will help you defuse your anger and understand your own feelings before you speak.

Let's face it, sex is an important part of a relationship. Maslow identified and categorized it as a primary physiological need. It was recognized even earlier in the Garden of Eden, by the first man and woman, Adam and Eve. It continues to be sought after to fulfill both physiological and emotional needs by millions of people today.

Sex is an important part of a relationship. However, the importance of sex during a couple's life is influenced by a host of factors and may shift at times. One of the key factors is the emotional commitment and feelings each partner has for the other. When feelings are especially warm and tender, a couple's sexual activity will generally increase in frequency and intensity. On the other hand, a decline in sexual activity doesn't necessarily signify a loss of love. It can be the result of physical discomfort or illness, pressure or anxiety, or even personal problems.

Nonetheless, a popular question among men is, "How can I become a better lover?" Nearly every man is interested in improving his prowess with the opposite sex. It's important to the ego and increases a man's appeal among women. Most authorities agree sex is simply best when it represents a sharing of mutual feelings and not merely a carnal act for the gratification of pure physiological needs. Sex is best when it is marked by mutual caring, concern, and a desire to please (give).

KEY INSIGHTS

The *Redbook Report On Sexual Relationships* appearing in the magazine's October, 1980 issue, provides insights into ways you can improve your ability as a lover. It reports on the findings from a survey of more than 26,000 women and men. Here are some helpful conclusions that may be drawn from the findings:

DON'T USE A SCORECARD: Despite popular opinion, orgasm is *not* the ultimate goal. In fact, the absence of orgasm among women does not mean they don't find the experience satisfying. About 70 percent of all women surveyed claimed that failure to reach an orgasm was "no big thing" with regards to the quality of the relationship. So don't get uptight about needing to stimulate your partner to an orgasm every time you engage in lovemaking. The more anxious you make her feel, the less likely it is that she'll reach an orgasm and the less enjoyable the experience will be for both of you. Just relax and share your love, and let it happen.

COMMUNICATE OPENLY: According to the *Redbook* survey, good communications between partners is the single most important factor influencing a good sexual relationship. This consists of talking openly about sex, showing your partner where and how you like to be touched and getting her to do the same. Unfortunately, many people feel embarrassed and are inhibited in talking openly about sex. This results from sexual guilt heaped upon us by teachers, parents, and the church, so much so that it is even difficult for some people to enjoy sexual activity. Nonetheless, you need to overcome any inhibitions you might have and speak openly about your likes if you are going to improve your skills as a lover. As an indication of the importance of communication to the quality of a sexual relation- ship, people who answered "yes" to the question, "Have you let your partner know specifically how you like your genital area touched?" were more likely to have favorable sexual experiences. So get to know your partner's preferences. Don't assume you know what pleases her. Be sensitive to her clues and don't be afraid to ask.

Some questions you may want to explore are:

- What does and doesn't she like?
- What, and who, usually initiates lovemaking?
- What is generally her presexual mood?
- What stimulates her sexual appetite?
- What are her fantasies?

And, don't forget yourself. Show your partner what you like. Don't be concerned and guilt-ridden with feelings of selfishness and exploitation. The more you enjoy the experience the more you will give.

It's also important to be aware of what your partner doesn't like, particularly when it comes to activities that cause pain and discomfort. Unless you find out what, if anything, causes her discomfort it could adversely affect her sexual appetite and your lovemaking.

THE CURRENT ENVIRONMENT: Vary your lovemaking based on your shared feelings and the current environment. Every sexual experience should not be the same. It would make for a very boring menu. As moods vary, so do sexual needs. Sometimes she may want you hard and fast. Whereas at other times she may want you to treat her softly and tenderly. So keep attuned to your partner's needs to make each experience a new and satisfying adventure for you both.

HOW TO GET WOMEN TO TAKE YOU TO BED

Nearly every man fantasizes at one time or another about women becoming so enraptured by his sex appeal that they're ready and willing to take him to bed and devour him with unbridled passion. Yet every man can whet the sexual appetite of women and even get them to take him to bed occasionally. The key lies not in resorting to Machiavellian techniques like plying women with booze or false promises of love. Instead, you can stimulate a woman's desire to love you by living up to a principle discussed earlier: give women value in your relationships with them. In turn, they will be eager to reciprocate, repaying you with freely given love. In short, you have to give unselfishly if you are to receive.

You shower today's woman with value by demonstrating that you genuinely care for her and believe she is an important part of your happiness. It is when you stimulate a desire in women to love you in the emotional sense that they'll become eager to take you to bed. Ways in which you can demonstrate that you care—and tear down the barriers that block intimacy—have been exhaustively covered throughout this book. They include, but are not limited to: being "other directed," touching, openly communicating your feelings of affection, smiling, using her name, and so forth. Be yourself, be "other directed," let her know how you feel about her and soon you'll find women will be eager to take you to bed and share their feelings for you.

In summary, you can develop lasting relationships with the women of your dreams. First, be on the lookout for ill-fitting relationships and end them before you become too involved. When you meet the right someone(s) give freely of yourself. Commit your energies to making the relationship work and grow. Communicate openly, yet sensitively, about your likes and dislikes. If you follow these principles, you'll get more out of each new relationship.

CHAPTER ELEVEN

NOW WIN
WITH TODAY'S WOMAN!

To enjoy success with today's woman, each encounter should flow (or appear to flow) spontaneously. A healthy self-concept coupled with a genuine interest in women forms the bedrock of a spontaneous encounter. Now here are some final thoughts on how to win with today's woman:

BE YOURSELF

If there's one principle you take from this book, it should be, "Be yourself." For maximum effectiveness, the principles you adopt in meeting women should be those that are most consistent with and flow from your personality. If you adopt principles that just aren't you, you're going to come off as being wooden and artificial. Moreover, the extra anxiety playacting will create will sap your energy, enthusiasm, and confidence, thereby undermining your ability to make out with a new encounter.

There are scores of invaluable principles throughout this book. Some will come easier to you and work harder for you. That's because those principles will be more in tune with your personality. Adopting those principles that come easiest will ensure a more spontaneous and productive encounter. For example, I'm a toucher.

I love people. I love to be touched, and I simply can't resist the urge to touch others. So, when I make contact I'm usually able to tear down barriers and get really close to women through the power of touching. If you're like me and simply can't resist the urge to reach out and touch another's arm or hand, then this principle is a good one for you to use when you come in contact with women whose company you desire. If, on the other hand, you don't like to be touched or don't enjoy touching others, then don't. Instead, exploit one of the many other principles in this book that comes naturally to you—whether it be a warm, friendly smile or the frequent use of a woman's name.

BE FLEXIBLE

There's no established, tried-and-true, win-it-all-the-time set of principles. What works well in one encounter may not bring you the same level of success in another. That's because each situation and person is unique. The key to success then is really simple. Be flexible. Vary your approach based on the situation, environment, your mood at the time and what you can learn about others. Stay attuned to the needs of women and be sensitive to their feelings and what they tell you. Let the principles you employ flow from the responses you get from others, as well as your own feelings. Remember, your approach in an elevator is likely to be different than your approach at a singles' bar. Also, your response to one woman is likely to be different than to another.

BE CONSIDERATE

Other people have feelings too. Today's woman isn't likely to tolerate rudeness, a hyperinflated ego, or adolescent behavior. Always employ the golden rule: "Treat others as you would want them to treat you." Be concerned with the feelings of the women you meet.

Give them a chance to tell you about themselves and listen not only to the words they speak but to the intent of their message. By showing consideration you make today's woman feel good about herself and you.

Don't be afraid to be chivalrous or gallant. As long as your actions aren't patronizing, you'll score points with today's woman. She's not looking for Mr. Macho, but someone whose strength radiates from sensitivity, caring, considerateness, and concern. Chivalry and gallantry show that you care and that you're considerate.

BE PERSISTENT

Let's face it, you're going to be rejected at some time or another. Not every first impression or contact is going to be viewed favorably by others. That's just a fact of life. Likewise, that doesn't mean you ought to give up at the first sign of rejection. Chances are you may be throwing in the towel before the inning is played out as a defense mechanism to protect and preserve your male ego. Jim's contact with Denise is an inspiring example of how "no" is not necessarily a sign of rejection, and how persistence can pay off for you.

Jim asked to look over the menu at a popular dinner spot while he waited for a buddy to arrive. He began to tap the table impatiently as he looked down at his watch and noted his friend was already thirty minutes late. He looked around the crowd and spotted Denise, whom he had not met, standing alone sipping her drink while she listened to the combo playing a sweet, soft melody. Impatient with his friend's tardiness, feeling he had been stood up and attracted to Denise, Jim got up from his table and walked over to introduce himself. They talked about the music, the atmosphere, the cold Boston night, and much more. Jim decided to invite her to join him for dinner. "No," replied Denise, "I've already had dinner." While another person may have felt rejected by Denise's "no," Jim was confident in his ability to make contact and was genuinely interested in her so he asked another way. "Well then, would you like to watch me eat?" he asked. "Sure," replied Denise to a counter offer that led to the development of an intimate new relationship.

Jim could have easily given up and made a dozen excuses for Denise's initial "no." But he didn't. He wanted to establish contact with Denise, so he persisted in his efforts. Nor would he have given up on establishing contact with other women had Denise flatly refused his invitation. Jim enjoys a healthy self-concept and enjoys women too much to give up and cloister himself. If he wasn't successful with Denise the second time, he would have gone on to other pastures. You can improve your scorecard of successes if you remain persistent in your attempts to make contact.

BE PREPARED

Learn the principles set forth in this guide, and adopt and practice those that are consistent and flow from your personality. Employ these principles not only with each new encounter but with your friends, acquaintances, and relatives. You don't need to wait for a new encounter to be nice to a woman, to touch her with a smile, to freely extend a compliment, or to share an amusing story. Practice. It will serve to bring out the best in you and prepare you for new opportunities. Practice will improve your ability to make contact and establish intimate new relationships with today's woman.

NOW GO TO IT!

You have all it takes to win with the kind of women you've always desired but were never able to meet, much less share intimacy. So go to it! Michael Korda in his book *Success! How Every Man and Woman Can Achieve It* (Random House, © 1977) says, "Never say no to opportunity. Hard work, the ability to seize the right moment, the willingness to learn from failure ... are the common denominators of successful people."

This applies to any endeavor, and that includes establishing relationships. Now go to it ... and enjoy the fruits of your labors!

BIBLIOGRAPHY

BOOKS

BACH, DR. GEORGE R. and RONALD M. DEUTSCH. *Pairing*. New York: Peter H. Wyden, Inc., 1970.

BEIER, DR. ERNST G. and EVANS G. VALENS. *People Reading*. New York: Stein and Day Publishers, 1975.

CARNEGIE, DALE. *How To Win Friends and Influence People*. New York: Pocket Books, 1936.

FAST, JULIUS. *The Body Language of Sex, Power & Aggression*. New York: M. Evans and Company, Inc., 1977.

KASSORLA, DR. IRENE. *Putting It All Together*. New York: Brut Productions, Inc., 1973.

KORDA, MICHAEL. *Success! How Every Man and Woman Can Achieve It*. New York: Random House, Inc., 1977.

KRANTZLER, MEL. *Creative Divorce*. New York: Signet Books, New American Library, Inc., 1974.

MALLOY, JOHN T. *Dress For Success*. New York: Warner Books, Inc., 1975.

NIERENBERG, GERALD I. and HENRY H. CALERO. *How To Read A Person Like A Book*. New York: Hawthorne Books, Inc., 1971.

WALTERS, BARBARA. *How To Talk With Practically Anybody About Practically Anything.* New York: Doubleday and Co., Inc., 1970.

ZUNIN, DR. LEONARD with NATALIE. *Contact: The First Four Minutes.* New York: Ballantine Books, Inc., 1972.

MAGAZINES

OLDS, SALLY W. "Do You Have What It Takes To Make A Good Marriage?" *Ladies Home Journal* (October, 1980) pp. 76-80.

"Redbook Report On Sexual Relationships." *Redbook* (October, 1980) pp. 73-80.

Index